## DAVID CHARLESWORTH'S

# Furniture-making Techniques:

# A Guide to Hand Tools and Methods

GUILD OF MASTER
CRAFTSMAN PUBLICATIONS

This collection first published in 2006 by
**Guild of Master Craftsman Publications Ltd**
Castle Place, 166 High Street,
Lewes, East Sussex BN7 1XU

ISBN-13: 978-1-86108-433-0
ISBN-10: 1-86108-433-1

Principal Illustrations by Simon Rodway
All photographs by Robert Seymour.
Except: facing page and page 142 by Wolfgang Busse
and page 96, by Anthony Bailey.

**Production Manager:** Hilary MacCallum
**Managing Editor:** Gerrie Purcell
**Editors:** Virginia Brehaut, Gill Parris
**Managing Art Editor:** Gilda Pacitti
**Designer:** Rebecca Mothersole

Set in Corporate

Colour origination by Alta Image
Printed and bound by Sino Publishing

# Contents

## PLANES

## CHISELS

## SPOKESHAVES

## SHARPENING

## FINISHING

## MARKING AND MEASURING

## TECHNIQUES IN ACTION

# Foreword

There is no sure-fire or guaranteed way of making successful furniture, but you won't go far wrong if you follow this universal truth - get the basics right then, with time and patience, the rest will come. Half the fun of making furniture is using hand tools, but to get the most out of them they need to work properly. Time spent learning how to maintain them carefully and ways of using them to their full potential will always prove worthwhile. Faced with a dazzling array of choice when purchasing tools, this book helps woodworkers to make the right decisions and feel confident that they are using the best tool for the job - in the right way.

I have known David for as long as I have worked on *Furniture & Cabinet Making* magazine and I have worked on nearly all his articles over the years. The thing that stands out about David is the pursuit of perfection and accuracy, tempered with a great respect for his craft. In this book he covers not only the tools and equipment that you require to achieve those giddy heights, but how to follow the unique 'Charlesworth' method. Follow David's ideas and techniques and you will get the benefit of his experience and insight - resulting in many happy, creative hours at the bench.

Colin Eden-Eadon
Editor, *Furniture & Cabinet Making*

# Measurements

Measurements are in imperial with metric equivalents. Readers should be aware that the conversions may have been rounded up or down to the nearest convenient equivalents. Where a measurement is absolute, no conversion has been made. See conversion chart on page 140. When following the instructions, use either the metric or the imperial measurements; do not mix units.

# Introduction

I am delighted to be writing this introduction to a third book of my technical articles from *Furniture & Cabinet Making* magazine. The first two books continue to be popular and I have been astonished by the amount of positive feedback from readers all over the world. It is very gratifying to hear that my observations help people to raise the standard of their work. This reinforces my belief that exhibition standard work is not beyond the scope of the keen amateur, once the basic skills and concepts are clearly understood and practised.

It is sometimes easier to learn by watching than by reading, so I am excited by my 'Hand Tool Techniques' DVD series published by Lie-Nielsen Toolworks. I think they are a useful adjunct to the methods described in my books.

Good results follow from rigorous stock preparation and accurate marking out. I am fond of saying that if these two operations are well done, we are three-quarters of the way towards a successful result. The cutting and fitting of joints is relatively straightforward if we work with sharp, well-tuned tools and have a systematic approach. An understanding of the face side and edge system is helpful here and I have developed the basic strategy to a more comprehensive level.

The quality of some hand tools available today is astonishing. We are living in a golden age of tool manufacturing compared to the 1970s when I did my workshop training. Tool selection is still a bewildering affair due to the number of choices available, so I have included a list of the basic kit of tools, which I recommend to all my students. These choices have been refined for over 30 years and it is not always the most expensive tool which does the best job. This list should help to save a great deal of money in the long term and prevent the frustration of struggling with unsatisfactory tools which do not perform properly.

I describe an experiment which you can do in your workshop that proves the necessity for relatively flat plane soles. It is impossible to plane a straight edge with a fine shaving if the plane sole is concave in its length. This chapter also describes a method for flattening and polishing plane soles.

Quick reliable sharpening methods are essential and I am a strong advocate of honing guides. These ensure repeatability and razor-sharp tools from the outset. I use a simple set of three Japanese waterstones, which give a superfine edge and hone more advanced steels, such as A2, without difficulty. It is particularly important to understand the possible pitfalls that stem from the softness of these marvellous stones. A hollow stone will do incalculable damage to the flat side of a blade in a remarkably short time, so clear guidance has been included for their care and use.

David Charlesworth, 2006

# Tools of the Trade

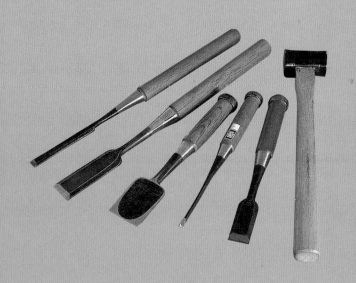

Use of hand tools is a fundamental part of making successful furniture. This tool list has been refined over 30 years and is always recommended to my students.

**Below: Jeweller's piercing saw.**

There has been a notable resurgence of interest in woodworking hand tools, partly as a result of power-tool programmes on television. These encouraged people to have a go, but they found that power tools did not always provide the best result.

Struggling with poor tools is frustrating, often leading the user to feel deficient in skill and competence. Good tools do the job with less fuss, making it easier to get the desired result. A poor tool will plague us forever, while a good one will give pleasure and satisfaction every time it is used. Another advantage of buying good tools is that you will only do it once, saving a considerable amount of money. However, there are a lot of quality tools around and the choices available can be confusing, so here is a list of tools that I recommend for furniture making.

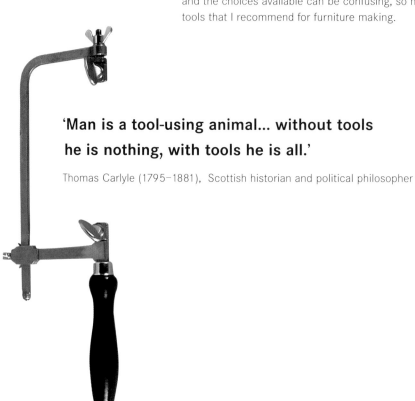

## 'Man is a tool-using animal... without tools he is nothing, with tools he is all.'

Thomas Carlyle (1795–1881), Scottish historian and political philosopher

# Hand planes

### Bench plane

Assuming you have access to some form of machine planer, a No. 5 or No. 5½ will do the vast majority of your work. The 5 is a little lighter and is long enough to keep things flat without the weight of a No. 7 or 8. One of these can be added later if you do much large work.

I never use the shorter smoothing planes, having decided to tune up my 5½ as a super smoother. It is used to perfect results from the machine planer, trim joints after glue-up, shoot end grain and fit drawers and doors.

It is important to persevere with and master one plane, before being seduced by the myriad of speciality planes. The Lie-Nielsen 5½ plane is top of my list, but if price is an issue we can successfully tune up an old Stanley or Record to give nearly the same performance.

A top quality replacement iron, such as the 0.095in (2.4mm) thick A2 cryo blades from Lie-Nielsen or Ron Hock, will make a vast improvement. These will keep you working for considerably longer between sharpenings than any others, and the extra thickness will help to reduce chatter.

**Above: Top left, tuned-up Stanley with A2 blade and thick chipbreaker. Right, Lie-Nielsen 5½, Screwdriver and brush.**

### Low angle block plane

I spent years experimenting with my 1970 Stanley 60½ low angle, adjustable mouth block plane, trying to get a reasonable performance. Hock or Lie-Nielsen 0.095in (2.4mm) A2 cryo blades will improve matters, but the Lie-Nielsen plane with its extra thick ⅛in (3.2mm) blade works much better. I feel it is not worth compromising with Stanley or Record, which are light in weight and have some design flaws. A good block plane will take continuous end-grain shavings from hardwood, without chatter. The standard angle, 20° block plane can be added later if you regularly work on small areas of long grain.

**Above: Stanley No. 80 scraper plane with Hock replacement blade. Hock burnisher and Clifton burnisher with card scraper and mill file.**

### Large shoulder plane

This is probably the only shoulder plane you will ever need. I find it convenient, even for small work. If you want to do secret mitre dovetails then this is the tool.

The weight is desirable as the heft helps the planing action considerably. I started with the number 311, '3-in-1' plane, but it never worked that well. If you intend to do curved work at least one spokeshave will be required. The Lie-Nielsen Boggs model, with a ⅛in (3.2mm) thick blade, is superior to Stanley and Record spokeshaves.

The Stanley No. 80 scraper plane is inexpensive, and provides a good introduction. Its performance will be transformed by the addition of a Hock replacement blade, costing slightly more than the tool. Scraper planes are only necessary for large areas of veneered work. They will smooth difficult grain, if you have not mastered control of tearout.

You will need a burnisher to form the hook on your scraping blades. Ron Hock's is excellent and we have also used burnishers from Roberts & Lee and Clifton.

**Above: Top, large shoulder plane. Middle, Boggs spokeshave. Bottom, Lie-Nielsen 60½ low angle block plane**

# Chisels

Considering the amount of use we get from planes and the investment we make in them, I can see no possible excuse for working with unsatisfactory chisels. A good chisel should last at least one lifetime, if you sharpen carefully.

For the last 20 years I have advocated professional-quality Japanese chisels, and I have no intention of getting rid of mine. However, the recent emergence of A2 cryo chisels superbly ground and shaped, with delicate edges and tough comfortable handles, leaves me with no choice but to suggest the new Lie-Nielsen range.

These are much more user-friendly for the Western craftsman as they are less brittle and easier to prepare. Incidentally, the Lie-Nielsen mortice chisels should now be available as well. The Hornbeam handles can be tapped with a metal hammer, and replacement handles are easy to make and fit if you want a paring-style handle.

**Above: Five-piece Lie-Nielsen A2 cryo chisel set and one fitted with paring-style homemade handle, plus two of the new mortice chisels.**

# Hammers

My favourite is the 13oz (375g) barrel-shaped hammer from The Japan Woodworker or Dick Fine Tools. The larger face makes it less likely that you will marr the ends of your chisels, with a stray blow. The hammers available here are very reasonable but with smaller faces.

**Above: A barrel-shaped hammer from The Japan Woodworker.**

# Sharpening

The edge quality produced by Japanese waterstones is phenomenal, and I think it is worth learning the very disciplined approach that they require. They remove metal faster than the other systems, and the initial cost is lower. I use three King (Ice Bear) manmade stones: 800grit (coarse), 1200grit (medium) and 8000grit (superfine/polishing). The Nagura, used for preparing a slurry, should be included with the 6000 or 8000grit stones. You can save outlay by using a 6000grit instead of the 8000, but the volume of stone is less. If you use my 'ruler trick' (see below) for plane blades, a cheap 6in (150mm), stainless ruler will be needed.

**Above: King brand waterstones: with a Dycem sticky mat, ruler and camellia oil to keep rust at bay.**

# Ruler trick

This is an effective way for putting a mirror polish on the back of the blade adjacent to the cutting edge. I use it for all edge tools except chisels:

Stick a ¹⁄₆₄in (0.5mm) thick, stainless steel rule to one long edge of the stone with slurry, then move the blade laterally, while propped up on the ruler, using a short stroke across the stone. Only the leading edge contacts the stone, and a ³⁄₃₂in (2mm) band of high polish is quickly produced.

# Honing guides

The 'Eclipse-type' side-clamping guide copes with the majority of tools. No one guide does everything, but the Far Eastern copy is a bargain and performs well. The narrow roller makes it ideal for producing slightly cambered edges, on bench-plane blades.

**Above: Honing guide.**

# Measuring /marking

Cabinet makers work to much tighter tolerances than other woodworkers do, so we must pay great attention to this group of tools. Although wood is constantly moving due to changes of relative humidity, good joint fitting requires accuracy. A change of a tenth of a millimetre (four thousandths of an inch) alters the fit of a tenon significantly.

**Above: Engineer's dividers are useful for dovetail layout.**

# Rulers & straight edges

The Japanese engineers' steel rules from Tilgear are well made, easy to read and a bargain. The 1ft, 2ft and 3ft (300mm, 600mm and 1m) cover most eventualities, though I still prefer the 64R Stanley rule for small work.

Please be wary of straightedges, where no tolerance is specified. Cheaper models are not good enough for checking plane soles, machine setting and precision work. I like the Starrett two foot, nickel-plated engineers straightedge No. 386. This seems expensive but will last a lifetime if you treat it 'as if it were made of glass'. The bevel edge is kept exclusively for testing, no veneer cutting please.

**Above: From left, Starrett nickel-plated straightedge, chrome-finish steel rules, and pencils. Dividers from Starrett.**

## Squares

Bench-grade engineers' squares are good value. I suggest a 6in for general purpose-marking of shoulders and checking. Tilgear stocks a 2in version, which is surprisingly useful, and the photo shows a delightful baby square from Dick Tools, in Germany.

**Above: These squares are from Tilgear and Dick Tools with Stanley adjustable bevel.**

*I have a grave prejudice against the glamorous rosewood and brass-stocked 'traditional' tools which occupy so much catalogue space. They are frequently not as accurate as you might assume.*

*My first adjustable bevel was a classic example. The sides of the stock were neither straight nor parallel. What's more, working on the rosewood to correct these errors could only be done once the brass had been filed back to allow planing. This explains why I recommend the Stanley model with the plastic handle. At least the sides are straight and parallel, which is the minimum requirement for this tool.*

## Dial callipers

Although digital callipers are becoming common, I much prefer this simple, lightweight, glass-filled plastic tool. The analogue dial is easier to interpret and its lightness makes for easy measuring.

This Swiss-made version is my favourite but it can be difficult to find. I use it for judging shaving thickness, measuring tenon thickness and many other jobs.

The birdcage maker's awl is a brilliant, inexpensive tool for starting and 'moving' small drilled holes, as in hinge fitting. It has a square-section blade and seems to have lost its proper name.

A good countersink bit and a set of cheap drill bits, 1–6mm in 0.1mm graduations is most helpful for small brass screws – 0.5mm steps are too big for this job.

**Above: Swiss-made dial callipers, birdcage maker's awl, 0.1mm drill bit set and snail countersink bits.**

## Marking & cutting gauges

The same caveats apply to these essential tools. The traditional pattern rules, and it appears that no thought has been given to the design for hundreds of years. My policy is to tune up the cheapest possible Beech marking gauges, which we get from Tilgear. The pin is converted into a mini-cutting blade, which will cut beautifully crisp lines across the grain. The stem needs to be square to the stock, so brass wear strips are unhelpful. I just turn the stock round so that its wooden surface can be planed and corrected. Four gauges are the absolute minimum, as it is good practice to preserve a setting until the job is finished. There are a few excellent gauges available, but the good ones are very expensive indeed. A pencil gauge is remarkably useful and can be easily made.

Marking knives are used against the square, and for transferring dovetails. A Stanley or hobby knife may serve for a while, but my preferred pattern is not available. The one in the photo was reground and shaped from a leather-worker's knife, it works for both right and left-hand cuts, and fits into fine dovetail sockets.

**Above: Marking gauges and a home-made pencil gauge with hobby knives and my marking knife.**

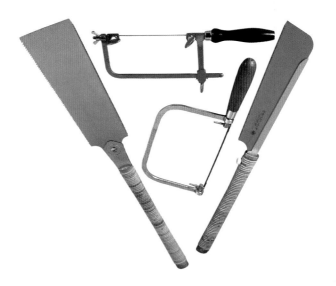

**Above: Jeweller's piercing saw and coping saw, Ryoba and Sunchild dozuki.**

# Saws

Personal preference and scale of work are significant here. I always advise my students to try before deciding. The only Japanese dozuki I have found, which performs well for hardwood dovetails, is the Sunchild from The Craftsman's Choice. The photo, above right, also shows a Ryoba – rip and crosscut – which is very useful as a knockabout, general-purpose saw. Both the Lie-Nielsen Independence and Adria Western dovetail saws work perfectly 'out of the box'. Roberts and Lee would be my next choice, but we should be ready to remove excess set from many UK saws. A saw will only track accurately, if it has minimum, even set.

We use a coping or jeweller's piercing saw to remove the waste from dovetails according to scale. The piercing saw is fitted with an 18TPI fretsaw blade to ensure efficient cutting.

**Above: Dovetail saws – Lie-Nielsen, Roberts and Lee, and Adria.**

# More advanced

As you get more advanced and confident in your skills your tool kit will inevitably expand. However, it is amazing how much can be achieved with the tools specified above.

I was intrigued to find that the invoice for the tools I used when I started my training in 1970 was for just under £85. The tools indicated here would cost over £1,000, but the quality of many items is infinitely higher than it was then.

I have not had enough space to cover ancillary matters such as essential personal safety equipment, clamps and general workshop tools.

# Planes

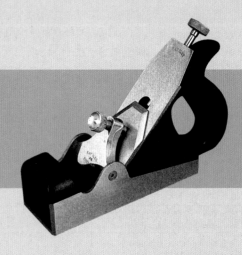

- Traditional vs Modern

- Flattening Plane Soles

- Preparing Chipbreakers

- Making an Infill Plane Kit

# Traditional vs Modern

The traditional and aesthetically pleasing infill plane is a classic of the tool box. This experiment compares its performance against the convenience of the modern bedrock plane.

Planes have intrigued me for a long time. When I started making furniture, Bailey planes were at a low point, with thin alloy blades, so serious craftsmen used to covet and seek out old British infill planes, which were generally acknowledged to be the best tool for the fine finishing of difficult hardwoods.

**Above: Ray Iles on left (closed handle), Lie-Nielsen centre, Shepherd on right.**

## Infill planes

As well as being aesthetically pleasing they had – if they were in good condition – a number of desirable features.

• They were heavy. The steel plates, sometimes with brass sides or gunmetal castings, were often stuffed with dense exotic woods, giving a considerable heft or mass.

• The blades were thick, around about ³⁄₁₆in (5mm). The cutting edge was cast steel, whether of laminated construction or solid. This combination of cast steel and thick blade is more rigid than the modern, thin, alloy steels.

• The chipbreakers or cap irons are thick and further help to stabilize the blade edge, reducing chatter.

• The mouth of a good example is very fine. This is part of the strategy to limit tearout, when complex or contrary interlocked grain is encountered.

• Norris, a London firm of plane makers, introduced a patent adjuster. This exploited a double-threaded arrangement to adjust shaving thickness.

The earlier infill planes did not have adjusters and to this day some argue about whether they are necessary. It is true that they are not essential as it doesn't take long to learn to make fine adjustments with a small hammer.

When these advantages were realized, collectors also got into the market and the prices began to climb. There is a limited supply and many planes have gone to the USA where there are growing numbers of cabinet makers.

# Resurgence of plane making

In recent years, the availability of new high-quality planes has begun to climb. There are a number of superb British infill plane makers – Bill Carter, Karl Holtey and Geoff Entwistle, to name a few. Various firms supply castings and parts, Bristol Design and St James Bay Tool Co. (USA), for example. Shepherd supplied infill plane kits for a few years, but ceased trading early in 2006.

Ray Iles recently introduced a welded-steel version of the coffin-shaped Norris A5, and his latest offering is based on a Norris A6, which has parallel sides. These are both at a price which might well be considered affordable.

# Bedrock planes

It was many years before I heard of the Stanley Bedrock range, and none came my way until I bought my first Lie-Nielsen plane, a No. 5 The bedrock frog is a great improvement on the design of frogs in the Bailey-pattern planes.

The blade is better supported on a continuous machined surface and the mouth opening of the plane can be easily adjusted without having to remove the blade. The seating of the frog has a much larger area of machined surface and the frog fixing pins are less likely to distort the sole of the plane. Clifton has chosen this arrangement for its bench planes, so we have two manufacturers offering planes which far exceed the disappointing 'Bailey' pattern currently offered by Stanley, Record and Footprint.

Both firms have realized the advantages of a thick plane blade, so we now have planes with similar attributes to the old infill variety. The main difference is the body. Bedrocks have a casting, while infills have a fabricated shell stuffed with exotic hardwood.

This wooden stuffing has a potential disadvantage which I discovered while building my Shepherd kit: the blade support surface is part steel and part wood; if this surface was completely flat when the plane was made, and the wood subsequently shrinks, we could end up with a blade that is not supported at its heel.

I am fairly sure that this explains an annoying habit of my Mathieson plane, where the blade setting alters as the lever cap screw is tightened or loosened. I have noticed that when the chipbreaker is screwed to the blade, it causes the blade to bend slightly.

There is demonstrably a demand for infill planes and I am keen to understand whether this is driven by nostalgia, or whether they really do perform better than a top-quality modern bedrock plane, the quality of these being infinitely superior to the Bailey planes which I bought when I started.

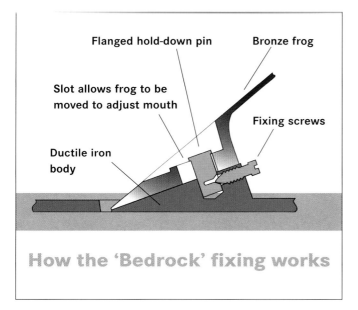

**Flanged hold-down pin**
**Bronze frog**
**Slot allows frog to be moved to adjust mouth**
**Fixing screws**
**Ductile iron body**

## How the 'Bedrock' fixing works

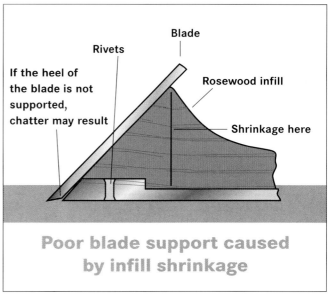

**Blade**
**Rivets**
**If the heel of the blade is not supported, chatter may result**
**Rosewood infill**
**Shrinkage here**

## Poor blade support caused by infill shrinkage

# Bedrock vs infill

To this end, I set up and sharpened several planes identically and at the same time. My Shepherd, the Ray Iles No. 6, a Lie-Nielsen No. 4½ with a 50° frog and a Lie-Nielsen No. 5½ with a standard frog. The pitch of the various planes was unfortunately not consistent, but the mouth widths were fairly similar and the chipbreakers were all set very close to the edge. I arranged similar shaving thickness by measuring with a micrometer while taking test shavings from a friendly piece of air-dried sycamore.

Firstly, I amused myself by seeing how thin a shaving could be achieved at full width down the edge of the board. All the planes took 0.0006in shavings and the thinnest I measured was 0.0004in. Apart from being good fun this is not particularly informative! Secondly, I set all the planes to a more realistic 0.001in shaving and tried some heydua or ovankol against the grain. The fibres were intersecting the edge at about 10°. Quarter-sawn heydua has a classic interlocked grain and we usually resort to double-bevel sharpening to avoid tearout.

The shaving thickness was then increased gradually until tearout was caused. I noted the shaving thickness when tearout appeared. To judge the depth of the tearout I reversed the planing direction of the edge and counted how many shavings it took to get back to a clean surface. My results are shown in the table.

You will see that tearout was caused at virtually the same shaving thickness in each case. The differences in my measurements are somewhat spurious, as it is not possible to measure shaving thickness to this degree of accuracy. The material being measured is compressible, and a considerable degree of 'feel' with the micrometer is required. It has been suggested to me that this test may reveal more about the nature of timber than it does about the planes. However, being able to obtain a clean surface while planing against the grain, with a shaving of 2.6 thousandths of an inch, is very impressive. I would normally stick to around one thou for difficult timber.

During this test I was really struck by the instability of the lateral adjustment on the two infill planes. I believe it is necessary to ease the tension of the lever cap screw before making shaving adjustments. Nearly every time I made a small depth of shaving adjustment the lateral positioning was lost.

The lateral adjustment is extremely twitchy as the distance from blade edge to the chipbreaker screw is significantly shorter than on a bedrock/Bailey plane. I have heard of this problem before, and the adjustment on the bedrocks is much easier. It is most unusual for a change of shaving thickness to upset the lateral adjustment.

## My table of results (with slightly spurious measurements)

| Plane | L-N 4½ | L-N 5½ | My Shepherd | RAY ILES |
|---|---|---|---|---|
| Pitch of frog | 50° | 45° | 45° | 47.5° |
| Blade thickness | 3.6mm | 3.6mm | 5.2mm | 4.0mm |
| First sign of tearout (shaving thickness) | 0.0024in | 0.0022in | 0.0018in | 0.002in |
| Considerable tearout (shaving thickness) | 0.0026in | 0.0024in | 0.0024in | 0.0024in |

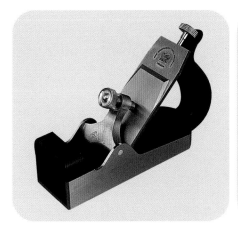 

 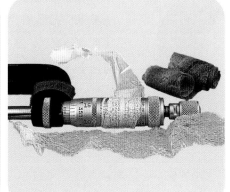

## Conclusion

To sum up, I can see no clear advantage of these two infills over a top-class modern bedrock, and I know which ones I will continue to use in the future. This may be heresy to many traditionalists, but so be it. Infills are a direct link to our cabinet-making history and are undoubtedly aesthetically pleasing. They work well and I doubt that any converts will be remotely swayed by my subjective opinion!

**Top left: My Shepherd kit with Hotley adjuster added.**

**Top right: Lie-Nielsen No. 4½ with 50° (prototope) frog.**

**Bottom left: Lie-Nielsen No. 5½.**

**Bottom right: Micrometer used to measure shaving thickness + thick and thin shavings – print can be read through the thin sycamore shavings.**

# Ray Iles A6 steel smoothing plane

This is a wonderful time for buyers and users of quality woodworking hand tools. The range of these now available is outstanding and seems to increase every year. How different from the 70s, which must have been the lowest point of all time. So, on to the new Ray Iles A6 steel smoothing plane.

This arrived, well packed, covered in rust preventative and with a few shavings of rosewood nestling in the plane. This demonstrated that it had been tested and the blade was well sharpened. I was able to take shavings of less than one thou, straight out of the box – having removed the grease.

The plane is generally very similar to the A5. The steel shell is of welded construction and the sides are parallel instead of coffin-shaped. The length of sole is 7⅜in, with a blade width of 2⅛in.

The overall finish is workmanlike and quite adequate for use. There is no unnecessary polishing of interior surfaces – a time-consuming abyss which I fell into with my Shepherd kit. Ray uses a 40tpi single thread for his adjuster, which gives fine control of the depth of shaving.

The sole of the plane is very well finished, with a minute convexity in length and width. This is an indication of the care that has been lavished on the hand lapping. The ability to take very fine shavings is a good indicator of sole condition.

The mouth was very fine, about six thousandths of an inch, which is excellent for fine finishing work. I believe that Ray will supply blades of slightly different thicknesses so that customers can have a mouth width to suit their style of work. The blade is 3.9mm (⅜in) thick, of A2 alloy and it is pitched at 47½°. This follows the Norris tradition and is 'half way' to York pitch, which is 50°. The hardness is approximately 60–61 on the Rockwell C scale.

The chipbreaker/cap iron is heavy and nicely made, with the front edge still needing some fettling. The lever cap is of polished cast bronze, which can be removed from the plane with a 2.5mm Allen key. This allowed me to check the blade seating/frog surface, which was good.

Chipbreaker edges almost always need work and it did not take long to remove the narrow square edge, which had caused choking when thicker shavings were attempted. I decided to hone the front edge at 42°, which will avoid any possibility of a shaving trap on this 47½° pitched plane.

The only other two minor points that I noted were that the edges of the throat had minute burrs on the steel sole – easily removed with fine wet and dry paper – and that I would have preferred a more acute taper on the tip of the lever cap screw.

## Conclusion
It is a remarkable effort to have produced an infill plane of this quality and at this price, and I would thoroughly recommend it to users who want the infill experience. (Ray Iles also has panel planes available now.)

**Far left: The Ray Iles steel parallel-sided A6.**

**Top: Thick A2 blade with well-shaped chipbreaker.**

**Middle: Side view showing lever cap screw.**

**Bottom right: Adjuster with 40tpi single thread.**

# Flattening Plane Soles

Unfortunately, there is no such thing as a perfectly flat plane and sometimes sole flattening is necessary.

Plane soles are one of my specialities – I have been working on the subject for many years – so I can confirm that, for accurate work, the sole must be flat or minutely convex in length and width. Concavity is not acceptable.

No manufacturer in the world produces a perfectly flat plane, and some are much worse than others. Flatness is an expensive and difficult commodity in the engineering world. Karl Holtey's planes are extremely flat because he hand laps them, 'better than 0.0005in', he says. He has discovered that this is the only way to achieve the result he wants.

**I have devised a simple test, which we use on all our new planes and you can easily repeat in your own workshop: will the tool plane a straight edge, with a fine shaving?**

## Sole flattening

Sole flattening is easy – if arduous – to do, but the improvement in performance is well worth the effort. If errors are large start with a 900mm (approx. 36in) length of 60grit belt sander paper, glued down to ½in (12mm) float glass. Check the surface of your glass, before gluing the paper down with spray mount. It is better that the surface be minutely concave than convex and the glass must be supported on a flat surface, as it will flex. If errors are small, start with 100 or 150grit.

## Test your plane

For this experiment, I used a No. 6 fore plane and a 2ft, Starret precision straightedge, Part no. 386-24, available from Bideford Tool Ltd. (If you have no precision straightedge, try comparing two planed edges.)

My measurements with feeler gauges suggested a three-thousandths of an inch hollow in the length of the sole, i.e. exactly to tolerance (by contrast, Lie-Nielsen's tolerance is 1½ thousandths of an inch total). I have found this sort of hollow in virtually every new plane we have had in the workshop. Stanley and Record planes are usually worse, with a pronounced bump behind the mouth of the plane. This bump is the result of sole distortion, caused when the frog is fixed down.

With a freshly sharpened blade, I proceeded to plane the edge of a ¾in (18mm) plank about 24in (610mm) long. The plane worked well and I set a standard shaving of about 2 thousandths of an inch.

After squaring the edge, I planed a hollow in the length by using stop shavings, until the plane stopped cutting. A slight hollow was produced. Next, a through shaving was taken to clean up the minute steps, where the previous shavings had been started and stopped. After one through shaving the edge was still minutely hollow in its length. After the second through shaving the hollow was lost and the edge became convex in its length – in other words, a bump. This is hardly surprising, as the plane sole is concave (hollow) in its length.

I keep meeting people who have spent hours working with 320grit. This is fine for polishing, but not coarse enough for making corrections.

Black felt-tip lines drawn on the sole provide useful feedback about progress. At the start of the flattening you can see how the felt tip is removed from the heel and toe of the sole, confirming the hollow in the length.

When all the felt-tip lines are removed at the same time, the main work is done and it just remains to refine the scratches. If you are working on a Stanley or Record plane, by the way, pay particular attention to the sole on either side of the throat.

Change the paper to 100grit and work till the previous scratches are removed. Then continue with 150grit followed by 180grit and finally 240grit. Next I scrub the sole vigorously with 0000 wire wool and metal polish. This reduces friction significantly and makes the plane slide smoothly.

## Rust is banned

Finally, I coat the surfaces with a couple of coats of car wax or paste wax, to help protect the freshly worked metal from rust and oxidation. Then, after use, I wipe the sole and sides with camellia oil to prevent the dreaded rust.

Castings do move and may continue to do so for many years, probably as a result of the relaxation of internal stresses. A plane that you have flattened today may well need flattening again in the future, but less work will be needed next time. It is worth checking a plane every six months and carefully observing performance. Any reduction in performance is likely to indicate movement.

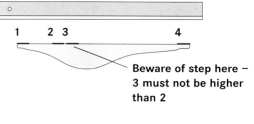

**Starrett precision straightedge**

1    2 3                    4

**Beware of step here – 3 must not be higher than 2**

1    2 3                    4

**To work well, areas 1, 2, 3 and 4 must lie in a straight line or be minutely convex**

**Slight hollows in the green areas are acceptable. The width should also be flat or slightly convex**

**Plane flattening technique**

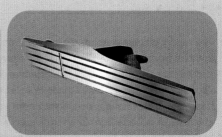

**Above left:** My plane flattening technique uses 60grit paper, spray-glued to ½in (12mm) float glass. This blue paper is zirconia alumina, which is much harder than aluminium oxide. Unfortunately my requirements are 'too small' to interest the suppliers.

**Above centre:** To start with, I draw continuous felt-tip lines.

**Above right:** A few strokes on the abrasive show the hollow in length. Felt tip is removed from the high points at the front and back of the sole.

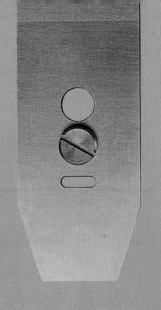

# Preparing Chipbreakers

Careful chipbreaker preparation will prevent problems of 'choking' and is an important part of ensuring that your hand plane performs to its full potential.

The hand plane can be a wonderful and accurate tool but, during hand-planing courses, students often have problems with blade preparation, setting a fine shaving and choking caused by unsatisfactory chipbreakers. A properly prepared, sharp chipbreaker (or cap iron) is one of the key elements to having a plane that works well.

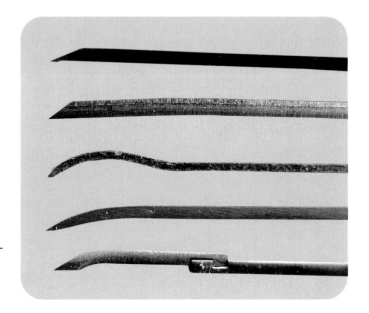

**Right: Various chipbreaker shapes.**
**From the top: new Lie-Nielsen, new Hock, Stanley,**
**Mathieson infill plane and Clifton.**

## New chipbreakers

Two recent chipbreakers on the market – one from Ron Hock and one from Lie-Nielsen – are both of heavy-gauge steel and should considerably improve the performance of thin plane irons. The Hock chipbreaker is well made from 3.5mm-thick steel. It has a simple bend and a well-formed front edge. The Lie-Nielsen chipbreaker is made from 3mm-thick steel and has no bend at all. This is unusual and should be of great assistance to smooth blade adjustment. Contact with the blade is arranged by clever grinding.

They join the familiar Record and Stanley type, which are thin, 1.8mm, and the thick Clifton two-piece model, 3.2mm. Infill planes have yet another form and are also made from steel that is substantially thicker than the current norm, often with pleasing decorative bevelling on their top edges.

There is a problem that I have occasionally encountered: for some reason the lever cap does not sit on the apex of the curved part of the chipbreaker. It could be that at some time in the past a different lever cap, or chipbreaker, has been substituted for the original, or the problem could have been built in at the factory. Sometimes the length of slot in the lever cap is too short. This causes the edge of the cap to rest on the down slope of the curve. The result of this condition is that the 'blade out' adjustment goes smoothly, while the 'blade in' adjustment is restricted.

We have also had several Clifton No. 5 planes where the front edge of the lever cap extended beyond the apex of the curve at the front edge of the chipbreaker. Adjustment becomes almost impossible as 'blade out' is restricted.

**Above: New Hock and new Lie-Nielsen underside view (left) top view (right).**

**The blade will not work itself into the plane if you set your shaving in the 'out' direction, an important rule that is often overlooked. Because of backlash – the slight looseness which occurs in any adjustment mechanism – it is always best to adjust the iron downwards into its final position. If the final movement is upwards, it is liable to work further up into the plane when you start to use it.**

In both cases there is a further disturbing effect. As the edge of the lever cap climbs or descends the slope the tension, set by the lever cap main screw, alters, and one feels the adjustment tightening or slackening. The flat-topped Lie-Nielsen design should avoid these problems.

# Chipbreaker preparation

In order for it to function properly, a chipbreaker must make perfect contact with the flat side of the blade. Inspect through the gap against a strong light source. If it does not, shavings will become stuck in the gaps and choke the plane. This fit can be achieved by careful work on the underside of the front edge. A slight clearance angle will ensure contact at the front edge.

The condition and angle of the top surface of the front edge are equally important, and the edge, where these two surfaces meet, must be sharp.

I have never seen, from any manufacturer, a new chipbreaker that was ready to use. The amount of work required to get them right is variable. Some can never be made to work at all because they are the wrong length (measured from front edge to the slot which engages the Y lever). Clifton manufacture two different lengths, but we are not told that at the tool shop. However, 'custom lengths' can be ordered.

**Below: Clifton lever cap, too far forward.**

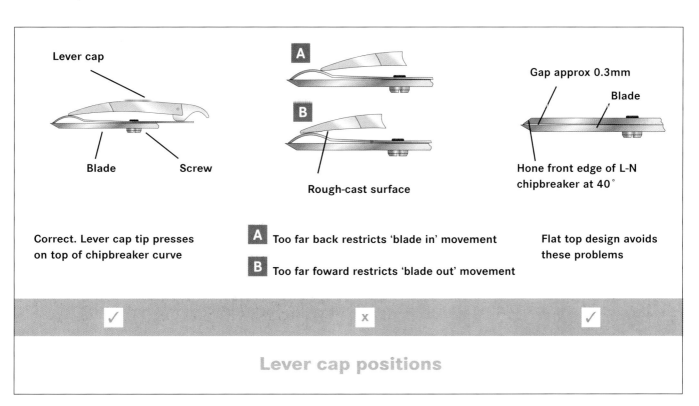

Lever cap

Blade    Screw

**Correct. Lever cap tip presses on top of chipbreaker curve**

**A**    **B**

Rough-cast surface

**A** Too far back restricts 'blade in' movement

**B** Too far foward restricts 'blade out' movement

Gap approx 0.3mm

Blade

**Hone front edge of L-N chipbreaker at 40°**

**Flat top design avoids these problems**

✓    x    ✓

Lever cap positions

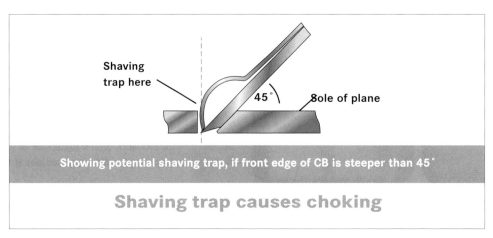

Shaving trap here

45°

Sole of plane

Showing potential shaving trap, if front edge of CB is steeper than 45°

**Shaving trap causes choking**

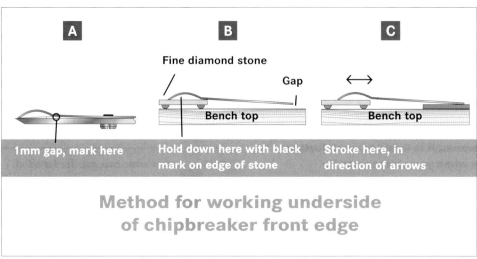

A   B   C

Fine diamond stone

Gap

⟷

Bench top   Bench top

1mm gap, mark here

Hold down here with black mark on edge of stone

Stroke here, in direction of arrows

**Method for working underside of chipbreaker front edge**

**A** **1** Mark edge of chipbreaker with black felt tip where approx 1mm of gap exists. This will give about 2° clearance.

**B** **2** Hold down with black mark on edge of stone.

**3** Measure the gap between the top of the chipbreaker and the bench.

**C** **4** Cut supporting stick to match gap.
**5** Use a short polishing stroke.

---

**Below left: Showing how movement is restricted by rough cast finish of lever cap.**
**Below centre: Working underside of chipbreaker, on diamond stone, with wooden prop.**
**Below right: Working top edge of chipbreaker in honing guide.**

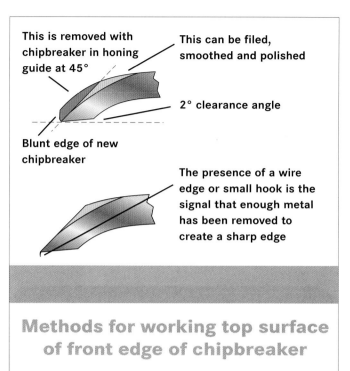

This is removed with chipbreaker in honing guide at 45°

This can be filed, smoothed and polished

2° clearance angle

Blunt edge of new chipbreaker

The presence of a wire edge or small hook is the signal that enough metal has been removed to create a sharp edge

## Methods for working top surface of front edge of chipbreaker

**Above left:** Working delicately to remove wire edge, no need to remove guide.

**Above right:** Final polishing, protecting the edge with MDF using 0000 wire wool and metal polish.

## Underside edge

Having screwed the chipbreaker to the iron, I look for a place where there is a small gap – say ¹⁄₃₂in (1mm) – between the flat side of the blade and the underside of the chipbreaker. A felt tip is used to mark this position on the edge of the chipbreaker. I then disassemble and place the chipbreaker on a fine diamond stone, with the black mark on the edge of the stone. Next I measure the space between the top of the chipbreaker and the tabletop. A thin strip of wood, about 3in (75mm) long, is cut to this thickness. The wood is used as a prop, to support the top end, while a small flat is worked on the underside front edge. A short stroke is used, only the front edge touching the stone. The prop is used solely to maintain a consistent angle, one that builds in about 2° of clearance. Black felt tip, on the edge, makes it easy to monitor progress.

## Top edge

I used to file the top edge, but noticed that students were inclined to rock the file and end up with a front edge angle of more than 45°. This can cause a shaving trap between the chipbreaker and the front edge of the throat. I now use a honing guide to hold the chipbreaker at 45° and work the top surface on coarse wet and dry paper, on a flat glass surface. The paper cuts quicker and clogs less, if lubricated with water. The presence of a small wire edge, on the underside, indicates that enough metal has been removed from the top side to get past the round blunt edge that we started with. I only resort to a file if there is a lot of metal to be removed. The surface quality is now improved to a polish, by working down through a series of finer and finer grits. The soft steel tends to produce a persistent wire edge, which is difficult to

eliminate. When I get down to 600grit paper, I work the two surfaces alternately; three light strokes on the diamond stone and a few extra light strokes on the paper. It is not necessary to remove the chipbreaker from the honing guide when you work the underside on the diamond stone. This method should persuade the wire edge to let go after a few goes.

Polishing the top surface will assist shavings to slide smoothly over it, so finish with 0000 wire wool and metal polish. Protect the sharp edge by holding it firmly against some scrap MDF. If you want to get really sophisticated you can create a slightly curved chipbreaker to match the slight curve on your blade.

## Less work to do

The new Lie-Nielsen chipbreaker has its front bevel formed at 25°. It is very well machined and will take much less work to prepare. I have honed mine at 40°, which will ensure against the possibility of a shaving trap. The Hock chipbreaker is also well produced and will require minimum work.

The Clifton two-piece is much the most difficult to work on as the short front section is difficult to hold without an aid. After preparation I 'glued' mine together at the joint with silicone sealant, to avoid dropping it. Thick chipbreakers will help to cut down chatter and improve planing performance.

# Making an Infill Plane Kit

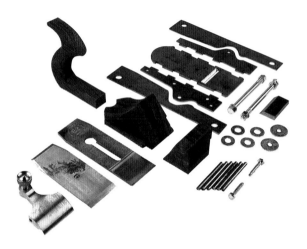

The process of building a traditional infill plane is a fascinating one, giving an opportunity for some nostalgic insight. This Shepherd Tool Company infill plane kit made an interesting project.

There seems to be a resurgence of interest in traditional infill planes. Collectable originals are becoming scarcer and more valuable, but I suspect nostalgia and aesthetics play a significant part, as the best modern planes can outperform anything from the past. My experiences in building a Shepherd kit will be relevant to anyone undertaking the building of an infill plane from scratch.

Hand planes are one of my major passions so I decided to have a go, not because I wanted this particular plane, but because it would be fascinating to gain some insight into the process. By chance, the only old infill smoother I have is a Mathieson (Glasgow). It is similar except for a slight difference of side profile. The kit is based on a Spiers (Ayr) parallel-sided smoother from the end of the nineteenth century.

## The illustrious past

Stewart Spiers was born in 1820. The son of a cabinet maker, he entered the trade at the age of 15. Although he did not invent the dovetailed metal plane, he was the most prominent nineteenth-century figure in its development. He is said to have built his first plane at the age of 20. His planes were exhibited at the Great Exhibition of 1851 and many were exported to America, according to Jim Kingshott in his book *Making and Modifying Woodworking Tools*. The business continued after the death of Spiers in 1899, almost until the Second World War. I am not familiar with all the firms who built this type of plane but Thomas Norris (London) – who added a patent adjuster in 1913 – was another famous exponent. His device controlled both blade projection and lateral adjustment, with one mechanism.

You will come across many dovetailed planes that do not bear the famous names. I have read that the cost of some planes would have been between one and three weeks' wages. Many craftsmen could not afford the price and built their own dovetailed planes, probably using a bought-in lever cap casting and blade.

Cabinet making relies absolutely on accurate measuring and marking out and these skills should be readily transferable to the marking and filing of a unique type of dovetail in mild steel. (Humm... we will see about that in due course!)

**Above left: All the parts of the kit.**

# Compound peened dovetails

The photograph of a Holtey thumb plane shows what the finished result would look like if contrasting materials were used (except that Karl uses a more acute angle). Steel dovetails and rivets should disappear completely when the filing and polishing is completed. You will see that sloped dovetails are present on both surfaces and pins seem to be absent. The side walls cannot be withdrawn, either vertically or horizontally from the sole. This is impossible to do in wood and is not the same as the 'Twisted Dovetail' shown on page 70 of my first book.

This kit starts out with rectangular 'pins' on the side wall of the plane and 15° dovetails in the sole plate. The edges of the pins are filed at 15° and a compound angle of about 5° (in each plane) is filed on the show edges of the dovetail sockets of the sole plate. Once you have fitted the pieces together and checked them, you can peen over the protruding pins and tails so that the excess metal flows into and fills the voids.

**'Peening'**
**This is a term used in riveting to describe how the steel is spread with repeated light blows from a ball peen hammer. This process permanently locks the three plates, into a rigid channel-like structure.**

The laborious drilling and filing of the shapes, described in Jim Kingshott's book, *Making and Modifying Woodworking Tools*, has largely been done for us, as the basic shapes have been cut accurately with a CNC laser.

# Some helpful filing guides

The filing process (and judging of angles) will be a great deal easier if you make some simple hardwood guides. I used a stick about 1in (25mm) square. Rout a ⅛in (3mm) groove about ½in (12mm) deep centrally along one edge. This should be a firm push-fit on the side walls of the plane. Cut the ends at 15° on a circular saw bench. Do be sure to clamp the work for the second cut, as the finished length is only about 4in (100mm). (Note that the opposite ends are mirror images of each other.)

I was not happy with the instructions for the second guide, which is used for the compound angle on the edges of the dovetail sockets of the sole plate. It seemed sensible to create a guide with a compound angle on either end. My interpretation of the supplied drawing (No. DE002) suggested 5° in either plane. The slot in this guide fits the sole plate and needs to be ³⁄₁₆in (5mm) wide.

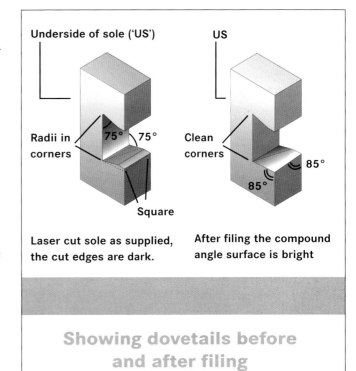

Underside of sole ('US')   US

Radii in corners   75°   75°   Clean corners   85°   85°

Square

**Laser cut sole as supplied, the cut edges are dark.**   **After filing the compound angle surface is bright**

**Showing dovetails before and after filing**

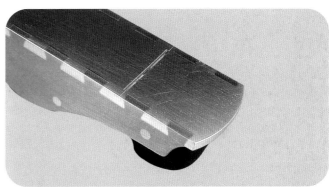

**Above top: The compound dovetails are clearly visible on this Holtey thumb plane.**

**Above bottom: Chalking a file helps to stop mild steel clogging.**

## Marking out

It is essential to know whether you are looking at inside or outside surfaces. I marked letters with black felt tip after removing any oil traces with acetone: 'RO' for right outside, 'RI' for right inside, 'IS' for top of sole and 'US' for underside of sole. The sides of pins and sockets were blackened so that it would be easy to see where the file had removed metal. As an extra precaution the slope to be filed was indicated on the visible edge.

## Files and filing tips

Files become blunt, like any other edge tool. Well-fitted handles are an essential safety measure. Blackboard chalk rubbed over a file helps to stop the soft steel jamming between the teeth. A clogged file leaves a horrible scratched finish. Files only cut on the forward stroke and firm pressure helps to make them last longer. The hand that grips the tip supplies most of the control. Files that are too fine to clean with a file card can be cleared with the sharp, square edge of a piece of hard brass. Use the teeth to cut the brass edge to form a perfectly fitting 'rake'.

## Corner cleaning

I was concerned about getting clean corners and knew that I had never seen a safe or cutting edge that would do this. There is always a slight radius on the edge of a file. Karl Holtey advised me that the trick is to grind a new safe edge on the file. This can be done at an angle slightly less than the corner that you are trying to clean. I did this with a simple wooden wedge clamped to the flat table of my Tormek grinder. The file was offered up to the flat 'side' surface of the stone. Since the plane is all steel, sharp corners are not entirely necessary. You could create a small radiused edge on the mating part.

## Side plates

Mount the side plates in the vice with the outside facing you. The part being filed should project as little as possible from the soft jaws, to minimize vibration. I found it more convenient to mount the side vertically as it was easier to see the surface being worked on. Using a good bench light I tapped the guide into position with a pin hammer and clamped it with a small G-clamp. It is important not to remove too much steel, as you can't put it back.

It is only necessary to remove enough metal to get a bright, cleaned edge, nearest to you and on the end of the pin. It is important that the whole surface should not be bright – if it is, you will have removed too much. I had to do the end pins with the work horizontal, as it was more difficult to locate the guide. The top edges of the soft jaws were used as a support for the guide.

The laser-cut surface is hard, but once you are through this layer the mild steel files very easily. Few strokes are needed for each surface. I used an 8in bastard file to do the main work and a little draw filing with a fine file to refine the finish.

**Below left: Jig used on the Tormek to grind a new, angled, safe edge on a half round bastard.**

**Below centre: Wooden filing jig in position for pin filing.**

**Below right: The finished surface on a pin side – note that the whole surface is not bright.**

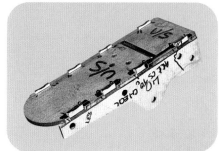

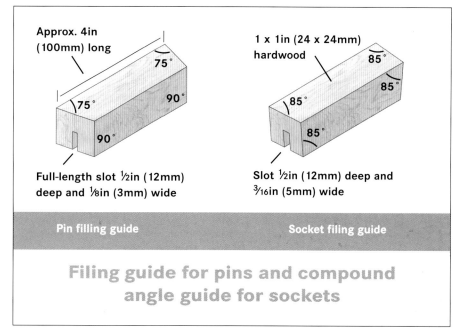

Approx. 4in (100mm) long

75°
75° 90°
90°

Full-length slot ½in (12mm) deep and ⅛in (3mm) wide

1 x 1in (24 x 24mm) hardwood

85°
85°
85°
85°

Slot ½in (12mm) deep and ³⁄₁₆in (5mm) wide

Pin filling guide

Socket filing guide

Filing guide for pins and compound angle guide for sockets

Top left: Finished tail surface – only part of the surface is bright.

Centre left: The shell with the dovetails fitted.

Bottom left: My oak guide protects the shoulder line. Shown with a 6in re-ground safe edge.

# Sole plate

This is done in a similar manner but with the compound 5° guide. See the photograph, above, of a finished surface. Again, please note that the whole surface is not bright.

# An extra straight-edged filing guide

Although the fit looked promising I found that the radius of the corners from the laser cutting was preventing entry. I was nervous about spoiling the shoulder lines when cleaning these corners, so decided to make an extra, straight edge-filing guide.

I made this simply from two lengths of oak, with a tight-fitting dowel at either end. Once I had fitted the dowels, I planed the top edge of the unit straight and square. I clamped each plate and positioned it between the oak cheeks while I filed the corners.

I clamped the existing shoulder line a thou or two higher than the wooden surface so that the laser-cut edges could be improved, as they are not entirely flat and square to the surfaces. You can see the guide in use in the photograph. I got my cleanest results with a modified edge, 6in half round bastard, changing the angle on the edge to suit the different shapes of corner.

I am plagued/blessed with varifocal lenses in my glasses and found it very useful to use a variety of magnifying devices for close inspection of the results. My students find magnification very useful for sawing dovetails and inspecting joints.

# Impressive fit

I am happy to say that only one or two surfaces on either side were too tight. This is a tribute to the accuracy of the CNC laser-cut parts and not to my filing ability. I used the trick of offering up the parts and reflecting a bright light off a sheet of paper to identify the offending surfaces (see page 78 of my first book).

# Drill the throat plate

Having fitted the compound dovetails, the next job is to drill the rivet holes in the throat plate. This ⅜in thick plate provides rigid support for the business end of the blade and should contribute to a chatter-free performance.

The throat plate is gently clamped to the pre-drilled sole plate. Use the smallest G-clamps you have or the drill mounting will become cumbersome. The aim is to get the 45° surfaces to align perfectly. Gentle tapping with a small hammer will assist in perfecting the position and a good light source and small straightedge will confirm it. It is important to centre the plate as well, so a couple of scribed lines gauged from the edges will help. There is a rounded front edge on the bottom of the throat plate. This is going to cause a discontinuity in the sloping surface but drawing suggests that it does no real harm (except aesthetically). There is not enough room to move the plate forward or the rivet holes would break through the back edge.

The photograph shows the clamping set-up, which was used to hold the assembly on my new drill press. I fixed a length of the bar supplied for the rivets in the chuck to position the work. The end of the bar is sitting in one of the pre-drilled holes in the throat plate. Once positioning and clamping were satisfactory, a centre drill was used to start the hole. Starting with a ⅛in drill, I worked up to ¼in (6mm) in several stages. Cutting fluid is beneficial when working mild steel. Please do not start with a ¼in drill, as the instructions seem to imply. There is a significant blunt area in the middle of larger drill bits that will generate a lot of heat and do very little actual cutting.

This job would have been easier if the rivet holes had not been drilled in the sole plate. Lining up a drill bit with a pre-drilled hole is not a straightforward job.

# Preparing the rivets

These have to be cut with a hacksaw, to length, from bar stock. It is important that the ends are square and that the length is 'two washer thicknesses' longer than the combined thickness of the components that you wish to join. I squared the ends against a disk sander and was advised to put a tiny bevel (0.5mm) on the sharp corner. This helps to prevent the flowing metal from splitting when you peen it.

In order for the rivets to grip we must also produce a small countersink on the outside of the holes. No dimensions are given for this so I consulted Karl Holtey again. He suggested using an angle of considerably less than 30° and that the width of bevel should be less than 1.5mm. The instructions suggest a rat tail file. I used an acute angled countersink, but Karl uses a three-cornered engineers scraper (see photograph, opposite page, bottom left).

Do not do the riveting until after the shell has been assembled and cleaned up.

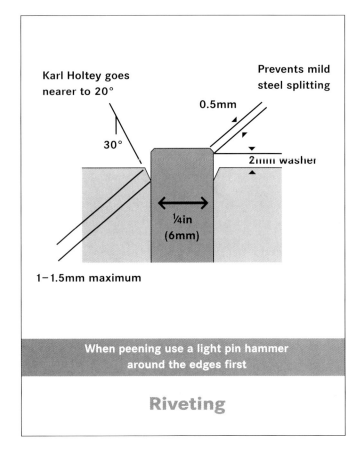

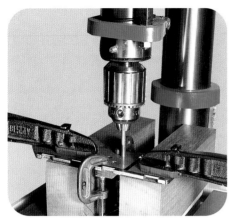

**Top left:** The set-up for drilling holes in the throat plate on my new Meddings drill press.

**Top right:** Prepared rivets in situ, protruding one washer-thickness from each surface.

**Bottom left:** The small countersink, which allows the rivets to grip, can be formed with a three-sided engineers scraper.

**Bottom right:** Fettling the corners of the throat with a thin file, not more than ⅛in (3.2mm) thick.

# Throat fettling

While the throat plate and rivets are in position (but not peened), we can do a little cleaning up of the corners of the throat. There is some residual metal from the milling of the 45° surface of the sole plate (see photo). This needs careful work with a small precision file. It is important that we do not damage the front edge, which will form the mouth of our plane. The file needs to be less than ⅛in (3.2mm) thick.

The 45° surfaces may also be cleaned lightly, though the final refinement will be done later. A buck block is used to support the shell during peening. I decided to laminate three layers of MDF with outer skins of maple, as I have no 3in stock. The solid outer layers will make it possible to plane the block, to precisely fit the interior width of the shell. Polyurethane glue was used so that no moisture was added to the structure. This will eliminate movement problems due to the loss of moisture sometimes experienced with water-based glues.

On an etymological note, the manufacturers refer to 'peining', but I can find no trace of this in *Chambers* or *The Shorter Oxford English Dictionary*, who only acknowledge 'peening'.

**Above: Laminating the buck block with polyurethane glue.**

Before peening or riveting the three plates together, I decided to polish the interior surfaces of the sides where they would be visible. The remainder of the rusty plates was also well abraded with coarse wet and dry to provide a key for the polyurethane glue, which is supplied to hold the stuffing in place. This unconventional idea is a good one, as it keeps the infills in place while the drilling and cross-riveting is done.

Blind holes were also drilled in the sidewalls, near the mouth, so that small brass buttons could be epoxied in. These buttons are about ½in (1mm) thick and keep the bottom of the blade centred in the plane body. They are not mentioned in the instructions but I have seen them in other planes and liked the idea. They will help to make lateral adjustments of the blade more positive.

**Left: The kit as it comes.**

## Norris style

I have decided to add a Norris-style adjuster to the plane, which may sound like heresy to traditionalists, and possibly the makers of the kit as well. However, I have had an original Mathieson smoother without adjuster for many years now, and have never 'made friends with it'. Whenever I finally tensioned the lever-cap screw after making adjustments, I found the blade always protruded a bit further than I had originally intended.

A fine cabinet maker wants a superfine shaving for cleaning up difficult timbers with minimum tearout, but the superfine shavings I set always turned into monsters at the last step. I never managed to figure out a way of setting a negative shaving as there is no way of seeing or judging it. This infuriating habit may have its source in some error of construction, but I could never pin it down and the plane sits silently in the cupboard, useful only as a conversation piece.

I get such good performance from my tuned-up Stanleys, Records and Lie-Nielsens that I have never felt the need for an infill plane. Part of my interest in this kit is to find out if there are advantages, other than nostalgia, to this classic type of plane. But of course, the answer will not become apparent until it has been in use for some months.

**Above right: Visible mouth area polished. Coarse scratches give key for polyurethane glue. Blind holes are for blade-centring buttons.**

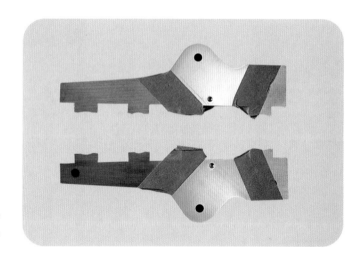

## Drawing and modifying

First I did some careful drawing, to find out if there was room for an adjuster. It was all a bit tight and the only way of preserving most of the handle was to lean it backwards a bit. This involved gluing a wedge-shaped piece to the underside of the 'stem' and re-cutting the top edge. When satisfied that the adjuster could be fitted, I returned to preparations for the dovetail peening.

# Cunning plans

Although moderately confident with a file, I was unsure of producing an exact, flat, 45° slope. My solution was to use the edge of a thick block of wood to support one end of the file at 45°. This angle is easy to work out. If the block is 3in (75mm) thick it is clamped 3in (75mm) away from the top edge of the back edge of the throat. Thin card was wrapped round the top end of the file so that the edge of the support block was not filed away. Adjustment of distance may have to be made for the thickness of the card.

**Above left: Throat plate in place but not riveted.**

**Above centre: Guide block used to file 45° throat plate.**

**Above right: Fitting infill to 45° throat plate.**

# Clever wheeze

The sole of the plane fixed to the buck block. The plywood retaining pieces have been left off the sides, so that you can see how the waste pieces of laser-cut steel support the side walls of the plane. This is a clever wheeze.

I have no idea how one would go about the peening without them. Note that the bottom edges of the waste steel protrude a little and will be supported on the anvil.

# Fixing plates to buck block

When everything has been lined up and you are sure that there are no gaps on the shoulder-lines of your steel dovetails, the ply-retaining pieces are bolted on and peening may now commence.

Good instructions for the sequence of hammer blows are supplied. It is a question of working round systematically, doing a little work on each pin. Start near the mouth and alternate from side to side, spreading out towards the ends.

This defined pattern is repeated many times. Don't try to complete work on one pin before going to the next. Occasionally turn the block onto its sides and give it a few blows to the dovetails of the sole plate. The hammering is done with the flat face of a 16oz ball-pein hammer.

Maybe my anvil was too small, but I had a problem with the whole assembly 'bouncing'. As it bounced, the shoulder-lines of the dovetails worked themselves apart. This perplexed and worried me, so I stopped work until I came up with the idea of gently clamping the assembly to the anvil before striking the pins. This was time-consuming but solved the problem.

I had trouble balancing the assembly on the edge of the anvil when I wanted to strike the dovetails of the sole plate, but in the end I made some simple MDF props to solve this problem.

As you strike the ends of the pins, the metal deforms and flows a little. The filed edges begin to bulge and fill the voids which were created by the original, compound angle filing.

# Finding solutions

Despite the excellent instructions for this stage, it is a nerve-racking experience for the novice. I do not feel I would have attained as good a result as I did without the extensive telephone support of two plane makers and I am very grateful for their help.

Some of the pins mushroomed-over alarmingly without filling the voids, rather like the top edge of a badly abused cold chisel or punch. Some filled and some did not. There came a point where I felt that further hammering would make things worse. I was advised to resort to specially shaped punches. Although these are given a passing reference in the instructions no details are given. I feel this is a serious omission.

Not having time to make my own from hardened silver steel, I modified a ⅛in (3mm) pin punch and a much stouter centre punch. The first was ground until the tip had a ¹⁄₁₆in (1.5mm) radius, hemisphere on the end. The second was given a flatter, ¼in (6mm) radius, hemispherical end. The technique was to form a small depression with the thin punch and then work sideways to encourage the mild steel to flow into an adjacent void – by sideways, I mean angling the punch to nearly 45°.

If a series of these small depressions is made along a shoulder line that was showing a small gap, it is possible to close it up. The initial depressions are made about ⅛in (3mm) away from the gapped line. If the surface is looking messy or too pitted, one can use the larger-radius ball to smooth things out a bit. However, avoid punching below the main surfaces at all costs, or the final clean-up filing will become very arduous.

I found a linen thread-counter, which I'm sure is similar to a stamp collector's magnifier, very useful. It enabled me to peer under the mushroomed edges of the pins and see whether the gaps were closing. Often they looked sealed tight to the naked eye, but magnification revealed small gaps.

The next piece of invaluable advice was to file away half of the protruding mess and repeat the punch-peining on every suspect joint. I had now probably worked round every pin and tail about 15 times – including the hammering – and was beginning to get excited about the possibility of a good result.

---

**Above left: Peening the pins.**

**Above right: Pins and dovetails with half the waste filed away, ready for second peening.**

**Below right: Using domed punch to fill small gaps. Note MDF props and clamp.**

## Filing and more filing

The ply-retaining sides are unbolted, but the shell assembly of three plates stays on the buck block. A good-sized bastard file, preferably new, is used to file off most of the remaining protruding pins and tails. Draw filing is recommended in the instructions but I do not see how this is remotely possible until the majority of the waste has been removed. I was very nervous of scoring the main surfaces, so used thin strips of skin-ply, ⅟₁₆in (1.5mm) thick, to protect them.

When close to the surface, I switched to a fine-mill file, and paper or card for protection. Eventually everything is draw-filed level and you can begin to check with a straightedge.

**Above: Magical disappearance of dovetails as draw filing reaches surface.**

## Magic

Magic is for once a reasonable description of the feeling I got as the pins and tails began to disappear with the final file strokes. I was advised to lever the shell off the block. This did not sound good to me, so I devised a gentler way of easing it off by dropping one end of the block from a height of about 2in (50mm) onto a thick strip of MDF. There was a matching strip under the opposite end of the buck block and the momentum gained by the steel shell gradually eased it off.

## Bad Saturday

You will have already gathered that I am not at all happy with some of the printed matter that comes with this kit. The photographs were awful.

Next, we are told to rivet the throat plate to the sole. There is a problem with access and support, and a large lump of steel – approximately 1¾ x 2½in (44 x 60mm) section – will have to be found to support the plate inside the shell. The assembly is very unstable as it is balanced on three rivets in a close triangular configuration. This gets even worse as you start gently peening them over. When the riveting had been done I was horrified to see that all the tight, flush, invisible dovetails had been distorted and displaced. The whole thing nearly went through the window!

More telephone technical support was urgently needed. My friends must have been getting nearly as fed up as I was. When I related my tale of woe they both expressed utter disbelief that the throat plate had not been riveted to the sole plate before shell peening. All that would have been required was a suitable cut-out on the top surface of the buck block to accommodate the throat plate.

Another disadvantage of the suggested order of work detailed in the instructions is that the 45° frog filing has to be done all over again, in an inaccessible position, because the riveting had caused the throat plate to fidget out of position.

They both emphasized that the peened shell is a delicate structure, and it must never be subjected to excessive stresses and strains. It only becomes strong once the stuffing has been fixed.

There is nothing for it but to plough on and hope that yet another draw filing episode will repair the damage. After some edge filing, further gap closing, and general tidying we can now begin to concentrate on the woodwork.

## Allergies, moans and mysteries

The wooden components have been milled, possibly on a CNC router or milling machine. Mine were unfortunately chipped in various critical places and the handle had a significant shake, which went about a fifth of the way through the handle. This was eventually flexed open, filled with superglue (cyanoacrylate) and sanded just before setting. Another shake in the blade support caused me to remove the overstuffing on the rear sides of the plane.

Here is the bit that I really cannot understand: if the steel plates are laser cut and the stuffing is milled, then why is the stuffing a fraction too wide for the shell? Come to that, the milled lever cap is also too wide by the same amount.

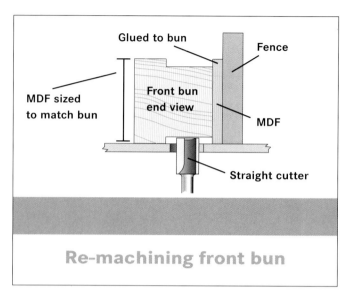

Re-machining front bun

**Beware!**
**Cocobolo stuffing is used in this plane. Every toxic dust list in the world has this timber high in the ratings. I discovered that I am violently allergic to it.**

Trying to reduce the width of complex pre-machined shapes is more difficult than starting from scratch. The reference surfaces have been lost and there is no stable surface on which to support the work. In the end I glued some skis to the edges of the bun to clean the base, and also glued a precisely dimensioned baseplate of MDF to support the bun while I routed a little off each side of the infill. I decided to turn the edges of the lever cap between centres on my lathe. This keeps the edges precisely square to the rivet hole on which it pivots.

When fitting the frog, I planed the 45° surface instead of filing it, for greater precision. The wooden slope was made slightly steeper than 45°, to ensure that the heel of the blade bevel is well supported on the sloping surface of the throat plate. The cocobolo stuffing is difficult to work. I used a double-bevel blade with an effective pitch of 70° that worked if fine shavings were taken.

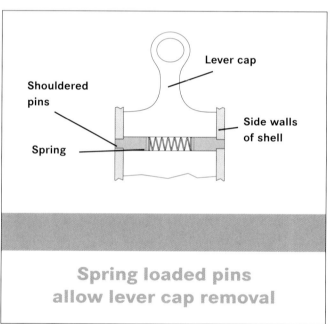

Spring loaded pins
allow lever cap removal

The opposite side of the blade, the one that sits on the frog, was far from flat. There was a major bump and a long time was spent improving it. The bevel was ground ¹⁄₁₆in (1.5mm) out of square and the surface grinding on the flat side of the blade was odd. I would have preferred the surface to have been skimmed from the start. Fitting the base of the handle to the radiused depression in the back of the stuffing was tricky.

**Above left: Routing the base of the bun.**

# Yarri Kanna

There is some very difficult blending to be done at the base of the handle, as it must flow into the large radius curve of the stuffing. This foxed me for quite a while, until I remembered how useful the Yarri Kanna, or spear plane, had been on some chair making many years before. It is very good at taking shavings from tight curves.

**Right: Yarri Kanna takes fine shavings from tight radii where handle flows into stuffing.**

Much filing, sanding and blending was needed on the handle. An elliptical section is the smartest. Being allergic to the dust meant working right in front of an early prototype of an ambient air filter. I found micromesh gave a wonderful final sheen after fine sanding. It is used for taking scratches out of plastic aircraft windscreens and is available from Tilgear.

A recess had to be routed for the adjuster and it was done freehand with extreme caution. If there had been time I would have used a template and guide bush, which would have been much safer.

The adjuster banjo is secured to the plane by two 6BA stainless engineering screws. I fitted a brass crossbar into a blind hole in the stuffing. The screws were drilled and tapped into this bar, which was secured with polyurethane glue.

The infills are glued in place with polyurethane glue before drilling and riveting. The lever cap is often riveted but before proceeding it is essential to check that the front edge of the lever cap presses evenly across the chipbreaker. To ensure the cap is always retrievable I used some shouldered spring pins recommended by Jim Kingshott. The final clean-up was done on float glass with a series of wet and dry grits. I started with 80grit and when flatness had been achieved worked down to 600grit.

**Above left: A Holtey, Norris-type adjustment mechanism.**

**Above centre: Wedge added to handle to tilt it backwards.**

**Above right: Adjuster fitted.**

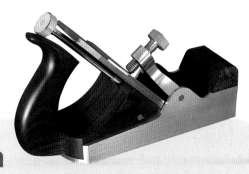

# Conclusion

I don't think I have space to delve into all the taxing details and difficulties I encountered while putting the plane together. A great deal of time was spent abrading and polishing. The chipbreaker was rusty, as was the blade.

The manufacturer's suggested construction times are not realistic for a novice. The manual states 2–3 hours of metalwork, 3–4 hours of woodwork and 3–4 hours for finishing. The time it took me is at least a factor of 10 higher, and that does not include my diversion into fitting an adjuster.

This is not a cheap way of acquiring an infill plane, though it is a fascinating exercise. However, despite all the highs and lows, I am delighted by the result. The first shavings taken were less than one thousandth of an inch.

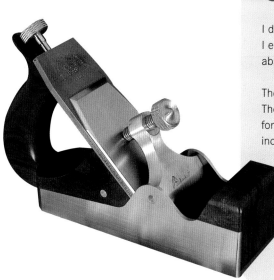

**Left and above: The finished article in all its glory.**

# Spokeshaves

- Introducing Spokeshaves

- Improving Performance

- Making a Spokeshave Adjuster

# Introducing Spokeshaves

Metal spokeshaves are notoriously tricky to set up and use satisfactorily. Here are some tips to help you tune up and improve their performance, also a versatile blade-holding jig to make.

**Above: My collection of spokeshaves, from left to right: Red Record A51; Black Stanley 151; Grey convex base; Kunz adjustable sole; Old Stanley adjustable sole; Preston; Lie-Nielsen Boggs shave; Lie-Nielsen Preston; and, in the centre, Clifton 500.**

I have found metal spokeshaves to be troublesome tools to use and this may explain why my collection grew over the years. They tend to be temptingly affordable in second-hand tool shops and I always hoped that the next one would perform better than the last. Preston used to specialize in these tools and made many patterns and sizes – straight blades with flat soles for convex work and convex soles (front to back) for internal curves. Some have a hollow-edged iron that is quite shallow while others have a smaller radius, both concave and convex. Chamfer shaves have a pair of adjustable side fences that can be set to produce consistent bevels on convex or concave work.

There are also many scraping, routing and beading tools that look superficially similar but cut in different ways, even the Stanley No. 80 scraper plane occasionally gets referred to as 'that big spokeshave'.

I propose to describe my experience with these tools in roughly the order in which I came across them during my woodworking career. I would also like to discuss the difficulties of sharpening and using them, as well as some ideas for tuning them up.

# Novice shaver

My first shave was the red, flat-soled Record, with no blade adjustment. The sole was not flat and had appalling deep belt-sander marks in it. These faults are easy enough to remedy by judicious filing and/or working the sole on wet and dry papers, spray-glued to a flat surface.

A lubricant, such as paraffin, WD40 or even water, will help considerably as you get down to finer grades. The liquid carries away the metal particles and prevents the paper from clogging. A suggested series of grits might be 100, 150, 180, 240. The polish can be improved by going further, using 320, 400 and 600, but many woods are abrasive, so mirror-polishing may be wasted.

If the front edge of the sole casting has become sharp, the arris should be eased with a fine file, as should the back edge of the throat. I find that 0000 wire wool and metal polish such as Autosol, rubbed hard after the final grade of wet and dry, will help to make the sole slick and slippery.

I rarely have to resort to the old trick of a wipe of candle on the sole. This is a great wheeze if the wood is oily and sticky and your ears are being assaulted by squeaks and groans. A few coats of good-quality car wax will help to keep rust from the freshly prepared cast iron surface, but a wipe of camellia oil should be part of the putting away routine.

# Geometry

The geometry of the metal spokeshave is completely different from that of most wooden shaves – they tend to have their blades mounted horizontally, with the bevel side up. A metal shave is in effect a very short-soled plane with the blade pitched at 45° to the sole and the bevel side down. Most have a cast cap, which holds the blade in place, and a few have blade-setting adjusters. One useful type has an adjustable front sole that alters the depth of cut without moving the blade.

According to R.A. Salaman, in his *Dictionary Of Woodworking Tools*, 'The earliest illustration known to us appears in Leonard Bailey's patent of July 13th 1858 for an "improved Spoke-Shave" which was an iron tool.'

**Above right: Adjustable sole spokeshave as seen from above.**

**Above left: Flattened and polished Stanley sole, one residual grinding mark showing. Note the excessively wide mouth, even with thicker 2.4mm Hock blade.**

**Below right: Adjustable sole type, viewed from underneath.**

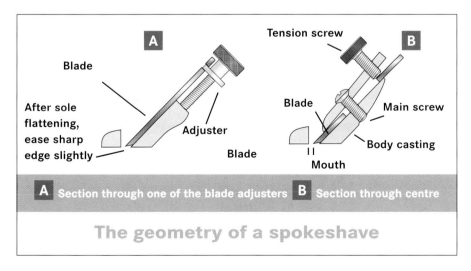

A — Blade; After sole flattening, ease sharp edge slightly; Adjuster; Blade

B — Tension screw; Blade; Main screw; Body casting; Mouth; Blade

**A** Section through one of the blade adjusters **B** Section through centre

**The geometry of a spokeshave**

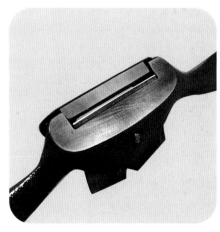

# Holding and sharpening

The first issue is how to hold the short blade, for bevel honing and also for back flattening. Flatting and polishing the back of a thin blade is not easy if you wish to preserve the skin on your fingertips!

I like to fix a small rectangular block of timber or plastic, just behind the bevel, with double-sided tape. If this is clamped for a minute or two the grip can be considerable. I flatten the back on an 800grit King Japanese waterstone, making sure to remove all traces of manufacturer's grinding scratches.

It is important to remember to work with the edge hanging slightly off the surface of the stone, for at least half the time. This guards against hollowing the soft stone and producing a rounded (convex) back. It will in fact produce a minute hollow in the length of the blade. The surface is then refined on a 1200grit King stone. I am increasingly convinced that nothing cuts as fast as the 800grit waterstone, but we must remember to flatten the stone frequently, on approx. 240grit wet and dry.

Frequently means, after a maximum of five minutes of heavy use. I no longer bother to polish the whole back with anything more than 0000 wire wool and metal polish, as I always use my 'ruler trick' on an 8000grit King stone (see page 12). The 'ruler trick' puts a narrow band of polish, adjacent to the cutting edge, just where it is needed. I cannot see the virtue of polishing the whole of the back and blades tend to stick firmly in the slurry of the superfine stone, by the action of surface tension. The photograph, below, shows a group of blades; some are satisfactorily polished and some are not.

**Below: Flattened backs: the narrow band of 'ruler' trick polish is visible on the Hock blade (far left). Old Preston blade (centre left) is very warped but useable. The Stanley blade (centre right) is unusable due to rust pitting. Note that even the Hock high-quality blades were not flat to start with. Hock blade for Kunz adjustable sole shave is shown (far right).**

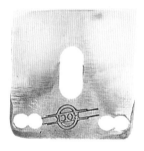   

# Grinding and honing

For grinding and honing, my first blade-holder was the archetypal block of wood with a saw cut in it. Thin blades were wedged into the saw kerf and I added a sheet of paper if the grip was not sufficient. The saw cut needs to be fairly close to the bottom surface and the front edge will need a bevel or it is likely to foul the grindstone. I like to grind the bevel at about 25°, then shape the edge and form a wire edge at 32° to 33° on an 800grit stone. This edge is polished at 35° on a superfine stone, say 8000grit. The final process is to repeat the 'ruler trick' on the back. This is exactly the same method that I use for plane blades.

**Right: Grinding bevel with simple blade-holder on a Tormek flat table.**

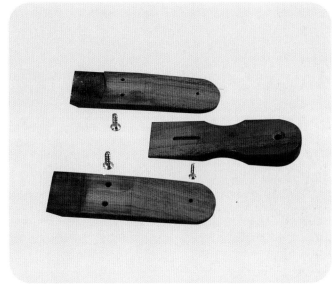

# Holding device

The holding device can be used on the flat tilting table of the Tormek grinder, or perhaps held in the universal blade jig. If you use a standard bench grinder please be delicate and check that the blade is firmly wedged, so that there is no danger of it coming loose. It would be much safer to add a bolt and a wing nut, acting through the slot of the blade. Two excellent blade-holders are to be found on page 66 of Bob Wearing's book, *Making Woodwork Aids & Devices* (see Further Reading).

My wedge device was developed from a delightfully simple small blade-holder shown on page 149 of Toshio Odate's book *Japanese Woodworking Tools*. His holders are apparently developed from jeweller makers' clamps. A useful feature of this type, is that it can be adjusted to take blades of varying thickness, it will also hold blades which have no slot or hole. I decided to make the wedge 'captive', as obscure items like this always get lost in communal workshops. The single screw at the back is left deliberately slack – its sole function is to prevent the wedge from getting lost. The No. 10 screws that provide the adjustment were longer than the thickness of the device.

They were drilled and 'tapped' in, right through, so that the threads holding the two parts together were substantial. The tapering, finer threads, with poor holding ability are sawn and filed off later. You could use bolts with nuts or wing nuts instead. This pair of screws has slightly oversized clearance holes in part A. They provide the pivot or hinge. When the wedge is pushed in firmly by hand the blade is gripped in the front jaws.

The device can be held in the blade-holding position of the Eclipse-type honing guides and honing projections worked out with reference to a simple angle guide. I continue to be pleased with this device and it gets lots of use, which is always a sign of a successful aid.

**Above left: The blade-holding device used in Eclipse honing guide. Angle board in background.**

**Above right: The blade-holding device in pieces.**

**Below: The blade holding device.**

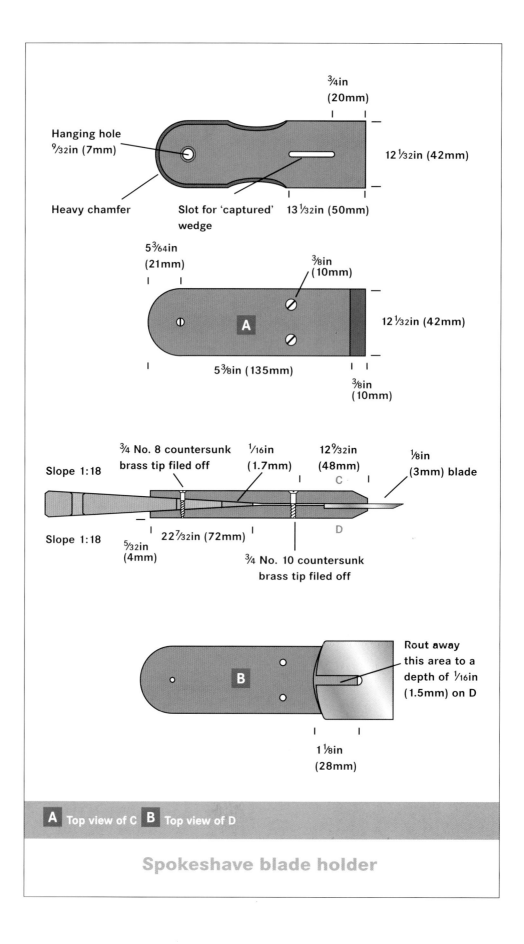

¾in
(20mm)

Hanging hole
⁹⁄₃₂in (7mm)

12 ¹⁄₃₂in (42mm)

Heavy chamfer

Slot for 'captured' wedge

13 ¹⁄₃₂in (50mm)

5³⁄₆₄in
(21mm)

³⁄₈in
(10mm)

A

12 ¹⁄₃₂in (42mm)

5³⁄₈in (135mm)

³⁄₈in
(10mm)

Slope 1:18

¾ No. 8 countersunk
brass tip filed off

¹⁄₁₆in
(1.7mm)

12⁹⁄₃₂in
(48mm)

C

¹⁄₈in
(3mm) blade

D

Slope 1:18

⁵⁄₃₂in
(4mm)

22⁷⁄₃₂in (72mm)

¾ No. 10 countersunk
brass tip filed off

B

Rout away
this area to a
depth of ¹⁄₁₆in
(1.5mm) on D

1 ¹⁄₈in
(28mm)

**A** Top view of C  **B** Top view of D

**Spokeshave blade holder**

# Improving Performance

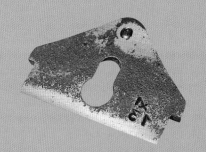

Spokeshave performance can be transformed by improving the blade seating, adding a thicker blade, closing the mouth, working on the cap and flattening the sole.

## Avoiding chatter

Chatter is that infuriating washboard effect, which I am sure we are all familiar with. There is an accompanying sound and vibration that alerts us before we have even seen the results, which look like single knurling on the surface. A low raking bench light will show it up to the best advantage.

I am certain that poor blade seating is one of the main causes. The bed which is supposed to support the blade, is often far from flat and many tools have a cast bed, which has received no further attention.

**Top left: Chatter – very annoying!**

**Bottom left: Bumpy, cast bed of a Stanley 64 and crooked blade back.**

To compound this problem the underside of many blades is far from flat. I think this probably occurs at the stage when the blade is stamped out from a long strip of material. Some have been ground on the honing surface but the back is still deformed. Colin Eden-Eadon, editor of *Furniture & Cabinet Making* magazine, tells me that a trick used in the Barnsley workshop when he was there was to insert a layer of veneer under the blade. This would have had two functions: a wide mouth would have been narrowed and, I suspect, that slightly compressible veneer would have absorbed some of the gaps between the blade and its seating.

## Slim problem

Thin blades are more prone to chatter than thicker ones and even the best tools will produce chatter if we set too thick a shaving. Spokeshaves are light, delicate finishing tools when compared with bench planes and there is little mass in the body and cap, to damp vibration. If you want to remove lots of material fast, a draw knife is a far better option.

Finally if your shave has a cap to hold down the blade – many don't – it is worth checking that the underside of the front edge is flat and contacts the blade properly. This contact may well add some stiffness to the edge of the blade when it is cutting.

## Improve the seating

I have come across two main strategies. The obvious one is to flatten the reverse side of the blade on benchstones, as you do on the honing side. Don't worry about a finely polished finish, just get it flat on a coarse stone. We can then work on the cast supporting surface to make it flatter, if it is accessible. Engineer's blue or felt tip will help to reveal the high spots if the blade is rubbed to and fro, and delicate filing or scraping, will improve matters. This is tricky, patient work and the marking and testing will need to be repeated many times.

If the blade is held by one centre screw, I think a minute hollow across the width of the bed will be acceptable as the blade will flex slightly as it is screwed down. The fit can be visually checked by peering under the blade against a bright light source.

Epoxy or plastic metal provide a radical alternative solution. I first heard of this trick from one of Robert Ingham's students and have recently seen a variation in an article by Brian Boggs (*Fine Woodworking*, October 2002 No. 158, p. 45). The idea is to form a new bed for the blade in a thin layer of epoxy which will be a perfect impression of the back of the blade. This also gives an opportunity to close up the mouth if it is too wide.

**Below left: Trued-up underside edge of cap: Stanley 151.**

**Below right: A trued-up bed: Stanley 151.**

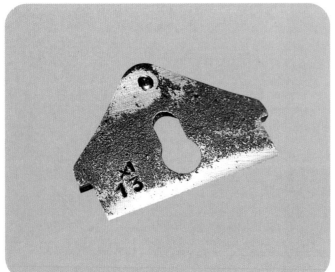

A thicker replacement blade is most desirable and a deeper bed of epoxy or plastic metal will narrow the mouth. I can see no reason for the mouth to be wider than the thickness of thin card, approximately ¼in (0.2 mm). On some tools the throat may not be wide enough for a thicker blade, but some filing of the front edge may provide room.

The bed area is cleaned thoroughly and roughed up with coarse paper or a file, to provide a key for the epoxy. The underside of the blade is flattened and the whole blade given a thorough coating of buffed wax, so that it does not stick to the epoxy. The blade is then pressed gently into the epoxy, with a sheet of thin card on top, to define the mouth. The blade should not foul the stem of the adjustment knobs. When dry, excess squeeze-out can be trimmed with a file or chisel.

**Left: This mouth is nearly wide enough for two blades! Clifton concave shave.**

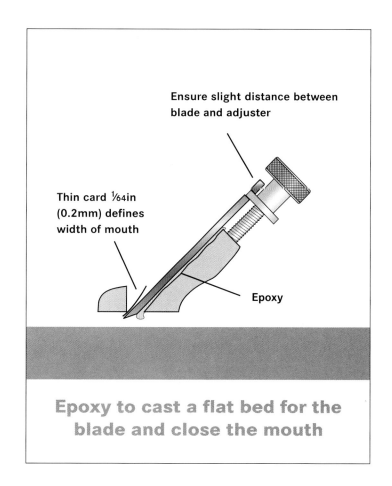

**Ensure slight distance between blade and adjuster**

**Thin card ⅟₆₄in (0.2mm) defines width of mouth**

**Epoxy**

**Epoxy to cast a flat bed for the blade and close the mouth**

## Replacement blades

A thicker, high-quality replacement blade will have a huge impact on spokeshave performance, less sharpening, a solid feel and less chatter, as long as the seating is good. For many years Ron Hock (www.hocktools.com) has been offering high carbon blades for the Record 151 and Stanley adjustable, as well as a slotted blade for the Kunz adjustable mouth shave. These are 2.4mm thick, considerably more than the originals. He now offers A2 cryogenic blades as well, which will hold an edge for four or five times longer. Ray Iles of the Old Tool Store has a nicely ground, high carbon blade for the adjustable Preston pattern. It is 1.9mm thick. A2 blades are also available from Jerry Glaser, P.O. Box 95, El Segundo, CA 90245.

The new Lie-Nielsen spokeshaves have the thickest blades of all, ⅛in A2 cryo for the small Preston pattern and the Boggs shave. These are beautifully ground and require very little flattening at all. Note that these two blades are not designed to fit other makes.

## Krenov's choice

The Kunz No. 53 adjustable mouth spokeshave is a modern copy of a type produced by Stanley and Preston (Stanley's first patent was in July 1858). The price is very reasonable if you get it from www.toolbay.net – I have seen it at nearly double the price in another mail order catalogue – phone them on 01 629 812334, or write to Toolbay.net, Bridge Street, Bakewell, Derbyshire, DE45 1DS. The firm has the whole range of Kunz tools from Germany, including many types of spokeshave, planes, scraper plane and a veneer saw.

This shave is the one that is favoured by James Krenov. It is not a particularly well-made tool, but with some work it can be transformed into an excellent worker. If you wish to fit a Hock blade it will probably have to be taken apart as there may not be enough space for the thicker blade. The hinge pins need to be removed so that the bed may be flattened. But beware – there are a pair of springs under the moving part which could easily be lost.

## Tuning a Stanley

Space for the blade is created by filing material from the underside of the moving 'shoe'.

I decided to tune up one of my original versions, which might be an early Stanley. The blade has 'Stanley Rule & Level Co.' stamped on it, but there is no way of knowing if the blade is original. The hinge pins were carefully tapped out with a fine punch and the springs removed. There was a mass of gunge and old sawdust packed between the moving parts. I found that the 1.9mm Ray Iles blade fitted well, requiring a minimum of filing, off the underside of the shoe (see photograph below left).

A hock blade at 2.4mm would have required some major surgery, possibly weakening the moving part. It was a little less wide than the original, but I wasn't worried about that. The blade seating was rough and significantly twisted. After some exploratory work I decided that the seating could be best flattened by working it against a flat mild steel bar with wet and dry paper taped to it. The bar was nearly the same width as the bed (see photograph below right). This worked very well and after checking and adjusting the mouth of the shave it was reassembled so that the sole could be trued up and polished.

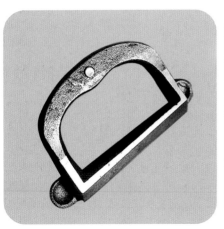

**Left: Underside of 'shoe'. My old adjustable mouth shave.**

**Right: This bed was trued by working on wet and dry taped to a mild steel bar, also showing 'shoe' of this adjustable mouth shave.**

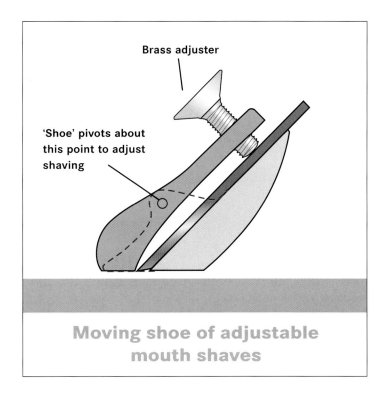

Brass adjuster

'Shoe' pivots about
this point to adjust
shaving

**Moving shoe of adjustable
mouth shaves**

## Set the blade

Blade setting is one of the trickiest parts of spokeshave use. The major advantage of the Kunz No. 53 is that the moving shoe controls the thickness of shavings taken. It is still difficult to fix the blade in the right position to start with, as it is with all shaves that lack adjusters. I like to adjust the shoe till the sole is flat and then hold the shave down on a piece of true hardwood. The blade edge is allowed to touch the 'setting block' and the main screw lightly tightened. With luck you will be able to make minor lateral adjustments with a small hammer, for a balanced shaving – repeat if things go astray. If a larger shaving is required try a cigarette paper or sheet of paper under the front or back edge of the sole.

## Shape the edge

Edge shape varies because shaves are used in two quite distinct ways. For rounding chair components and working bevels on an edge, a straight edge set slightly cocked has some advantages. Assuming the shavings taken are narrow we can choose whether to use the coarse side or the fine side. Rough the work down with the coarse side and polish it with the fine side.

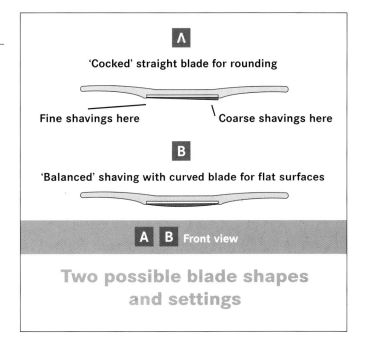

**A**

'Cocked' straight blade for rounding

Fine shavings here          Coarse shavings here

**B**

'Balanced' shaving with curved blade for flat surfaces

**A** **B** Front view

**Two possible blade shapes
and settings**

If you are working on wider surfaces or wishing to square up a curved edge, I think that a slightly cambered blade edge, set as a balanced shaving, will be better. A wide surface can be worked as a 'set of shavings' and edges are squared in the same manner as edge planing for a glue joint.

## Skew the tool

I use skewing strategies. No matter how good the tool and how well tuned it is, the tendency to chatter is still evident. I find that shavings of one to two thousandths of an inch work best. I also skew the tool alternately to the left and right while working. This lowers effective pitch and increases the effective length of the sole. We want to prevent the short soled 'plane' following undulations and skewing helps the shave to bridge ripples.

## Cap as a chipbreaker

Years ago I decided to move the cap of a 151 shave forward so that the leading edge was close to the cutting edge of the blade. The top surface was filed and polished to mimic the function of a chipbreaker (cap iron) on a bench plane blade. This approach is advocated by Brian Boggs, who replaces a standard cap with a solid brass one made from ¼in (6mm) brass bar. The two new Lie-Nielsen shaves have this feature built in and the polished front edge of the caps are set about 40 thou from the blade edge.

I was interested to note the quality and position of the cap on my old Preston shave as compared with two awful current ones by Stanley and Kunz.

## The ultimate spokeshave

The new Lie-Nielsen Boggs spokeshave has every tune-up feature one could wish for, built in at the factory – a precisely machined bed, thick, hard, high-quality A2 cryo blade, fine mouth and heavy cap which acts as a chipbreaker. The blade is pitched at 40°. Naturally this is reflected in the cost, but what a joy to have a tool that is almost ready to use, without hours of remedial work and purchase of replacement blades.

The one feature missing is fine blade adjustment. I suspect that this will not bother country chair makers but might be more of an issue for cabinet makers.

**Note quality of modern Kunz No. 65 (above) compared with old Preston caps (below).**

# My clip-on fine adjuster

To solve this minor problem I decided to build a detachable, external, fine adjuster, which is quickly clamped to the blade and removed when setting is complete.

Essentially this is a beam of hardwood clamped to the blade (there are two pins at the back of a trench against which the blade registers). The two 6BA bolts with knurled brass knobs are tapped crosswise through the beam and the ends make contact with the body of the shave.

**Below: Blade setting using my adjuster, top view.**

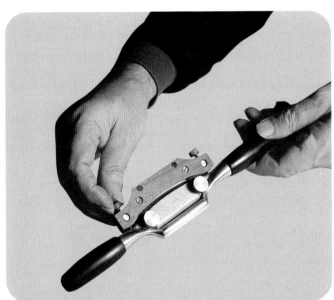

## Method

The device is clamped to the blade, which has been set in the tool with too much blade showing (the cap is not fully tightened). When the knurled knobs are turned clockwise, the blade is slowly retracted to its final setting (6BA thread has a very fine pitch). I test the shaving with a thin scrap of wood, fully tightening the cap when satisfied.

I am delighted to report that the device works really well. I now feel that I have a shave that will tackle the most demanding work with authority and control.

**Above: Lie-Nielsen cap with polished front edge that acts as a chipbreaker. My 151 cap was similarly modified many years ago.**

**Below left: Underside view of my adjuster.**

**Below right: Lie-Nielsen Boggs shave showing well-machined bed.**

# Making a Spokeshave Adjuster

This spokeshave adjuster is particularly valuable to furniture makers as it provides a reliable way of achieving the finest finishing cuts on wide surfaces and for squaring edges.

I n this chapter I explain how I made a fine adjuster for the Lie-Nielsen 'Boggs' spokeshaves, as I wanted a reliable method of setting fine, balanced, shavings with a slightly curved blade. This is an important set-up in furniture making, both for squaring edges and for working 'sets of shavings' across wide surfaces.

Like so many design ideas, it was conceived in a few minutes with a couple of rough sketches. However, the working out, dimensions and making took a considerable time.

---

**Below: Spokeshaves can be difficult tools to tame and a workshop-made adjuster can make all the difference.**

**Above: Exploded view of the components.
Note test holes in waste.**

# How does it work?

The device is clamped to the blade with the knurled knobs and clamping plate. The blade sits snugly in a close-fitting dado and the top of the blade registers against the two short screws labelled 'S' on the drawing on page 59.

Start with the blade extended too far. The tips of the screws – 'A' on the drawing – act against the edge of the bronze handles. As you turn the screws clockwise the blade is retracted (the cap knobs are not tight). By working the left and right side alternately, you can wind the blade back to the desired setting, tighten the cap knobs fully, remove the adjuster and away we go. I find it easy to set shavings of about one thousandth of an inch, and I prefer these for final finishing. You avoid chatter, get the least tearout and the best polished surface.

**Right: The adjuster before shaping – top view.**

# Materials

I used African Pau Rosa, which is an exceptionally hard, dense, rosewood-like species. Any timber with similar properties would do, such as rosewood, box or ebony.

I bought the one-inch 6BA CSK head stainless screws from GLR Distributors Ltd, a model engineering supplier that deals in small quantities of all sorts of useful things. I also get 1ft (305mm) lengths of hard brass rod and flat section from them, which are ideal for making smart mirror or hanging plates for cabinets.

# Warning

You can do small 'turning' jobs in a pillar drill chuck with files, but please make sure they have proper handles attached. The tang of a file driven into a wrist is a very serious accident.

# Knobs

The knurled knobs were made on my Myford Super 7 lathe. If you do not have access to a lathe or an engineer friend, it is worth looking at page 150 of Bob Wearing's book *The Resourceful Woodworker* (sadly now out of print), or page 212 of *Making Woodwork Aids & Devices* (see Further Reading), where you will see methods for homemade wood or perspex knobs.

I tap engineering screws into dense hardwood. Although some might frown on this practice it can be extremely useful if used with discretion. If the screw is not going to be removed frequently and is given plenty of length it will result in an excellent grip. I frequently use BA screws for small knife-hinges and stayed box hinges, because of the virtual disappearance of low-numbered, long, conventional brass wood screws on the market.

Tap and tap wrench. You will need a 'second' or 'taper' tap to match the thread of your screws and a small tap wrench to drive it with. These are both available from GLR. The hard steel tap cuts threads in wood or brass. When tapping metal, go one turn forward and half a turn back. The half turn back is important as it breaks the curl of swarf – if you omit the 'back' half turn, the tap may jam and break.

**Far left: The underside view of my adjuster.**

**Left: Blade-setting using my adjuster.**

# Making

Bandsaw off a ¾in (5mm) thick slice and prepare the two sticks, well over-length. Mark and form the blade dado first. Saw and chisel to remove the majority and use a router table to perfect the depth. Pare the ends with a sharp chisel. Form the clamping plate dado next in a similar fashion. Then crosscut the clamping plate and shoot to a good lengthways fit.

Now mark out all hole centres, referring to the labelled diagram. Holes 'B' are blind for the brass rod inserts, which are later glued in with epoxy or superglue. Drill a ¾in (1mm) hole through the bottom of the blind hole, to avoid the 'piston' effect and allow excess glue to escape. Brass inserts are desirable, as shallow threads in wood might wear out with extended use. In my device I drilled the tapping holes 'AJ' at a slight angle, after gluing the inserts. I did this by clamping the work to a wooden fence with an angled edge.

Note that the tips of adjuster screws 'AJ' must contact the circumference of the bronze handles reasonably square. It would be wise to have some softwood scrap components to check this with. Polished castings are bound to vary.

Drill tapping holes 'C' through the device and clamping plate. Now enlarge the clamping plate holes to clearance size. Drill tapping holes 'S' through the device only – not the clamping plate. Holes 'C' and 'S' are countersunk to the depth of the screw head on the top surface only.

Now you can cut the profile of the device and clamping plate and smooth them on a bobbin sander, easing the sharp edges.

Holes 'C', 'S' and 'AJ' are tapped, screws 'S' and 'C' are shortened to lengths shown on main working drawing and driven tightly into their threaded holes.

Fasten the tapped adjuster knob to its screw by high torque and epoxy, then install it and the device will be ready to use. I would love to hear from anyone who builds or improves on this design.

**Below: The spokeshave in its standard form.**

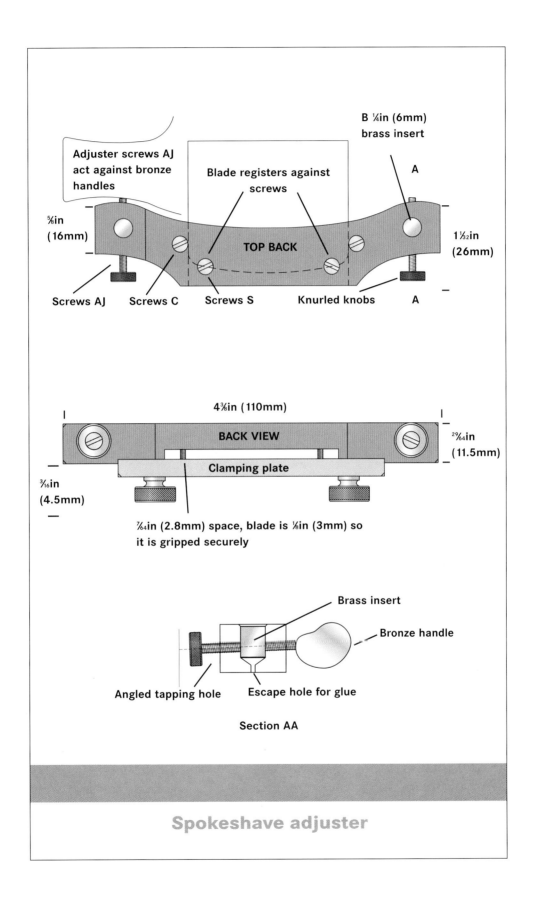

Adjuster screws AJ act against bronze handles

Blade registers against screws

B ¼in (6mm) brass insert

A

⅝in (16mm)

TOP BACK

1½in (26mm)

Screws AJ    Screws C    Screws S    Knurled knobs    A

4⅜in (110mm)

BACK VIEW

2%₄in (11.5mm)

Clamping plate

³⁄₁₆in (4.5mm)

%₄in (2.8mm) space, blade is ⅛in (3mm) so it is gripped securely

Brass insert

Bronze handle

Angled tapping hole    Escape hole for glue

Section AA

Spokeshave adjuster

# Chisels

- Cutting Edge Chisels

# Cutting Edge Chisels

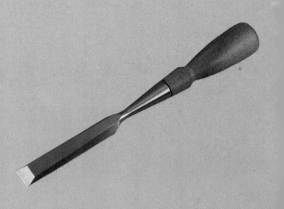

The eagerly anticipated new generation of A2 cryogenically treated chisels have arrived from Lie-Nielsen and have proved themselves perfect for furniture makers.

There has been a new development in chisel making, the first for many years. Chisels made from A2 cryogenically treated steel have arrived – I am very excited!

The improvement in plane blade performance obtained from this material has cut my sharpening time by a factor of four, and I can see no reason why this shouldn't apply to these new chisels as well.

## My first chisels

When I started my training in 1972, my first set of chisels were Stanleys, with their blue plastic handles. These were nicely ground and performed reasonably well in medium English hardwoods. A year in, I started working with some harder exotic woods, and began to notice the limitations of these alloy chisels. They were not hard enough to handle the end-grain paring and chopping of the partridge wood I was using to make cock beads on my sofa table.

In fact, it would not be an exaggeration to say the edge was folding up during the first cut. It was clear the major manufacturers were aiming at the site carpenter, joiner and amateur, the mass market rather than specialized cabinet makers. But to be fair, there weren't many cabinet makers left.

**Top right: A new, eagerly awaited Lie-Nielsen chisel.**

**Bottom right: A blue-handled Stanley chisel from the early 1970s.**

## Sophisticated taste

Matthew Burt was also starting his career at about this time. He left college with a classic set of new, English boxwood-handled chisels, but noticed he was spending a lot of time sharpening them.

He tells me a Frenchman, with a more sophisticated taste in tools, advised him to find pre-war cast steel chisels by good makers. The difficulty was to find ones where the back was flat and not too pitted by rust. I was not lucky enough to be in an area with a tradition of cabinet making, and was unable to find ones in decent condition.

However, Matthew is very fond of his, and has never found a need to change them. They grind and hone easily, and are hard enough for his work. He also says his skilled craftsmen are divided in their choice of chisels, according to what they have used in the past.

Half go for old cast steel and half for Japanese chisels. When my first student was with me, we found James Krenov's book to be a great source of technique and design ideas. He was using Japanese chisels and found them to be superior. When they first became available in the UK we were keen to try them out. They were a revelation as the steel was much harder than my Stanleys.

Once we had honed them at appropriate angles for hardwood, learned to cut in a straight line and never lever, they performed wonderfully well. It's significant that Jim Kingshott, who was a traditional, apprentice-trained, cabinet maker, took to them so enthusiastically.

**Above: The stamp on an old cast-steel gouge.**

## Pitfalls

There are unfortunately, numerous pitfalls for the unwary, and I must have fallen into most of them over the last 20 years. The range of choice is bewilderingly complex. The cheapest chisels are horrible, and it is important to chose workmanlike professional grades. Above this level there are many more, ever increasingly expensive, chisels.

These range all the way up to 'museum' quality, made by a few mostly ageing blacksmiths. It seems a Japanese blacksmith is not considered to have mastered his trade until he has practised for at least 30 or 40 years! In my opinion, these tools represent the peak of the blacksmith's art and are directly descended from the Samurai sword-making tradition.

**Top: Suminagashi chisels by Iyori, an example from a co-operative foundry, a Nishiki and a Tasai – note the laminated construction and how the two layers show in the bevel.**

**Bottom: A cheap Japanese chisel (top) and a well-ground professional-grade example from Mike Hancock of Classic Hand Tools.**

# Hardness

The performance of Japanese chisels in dense exotic woods is a result of the extra hardness of the thin carbon steel layer which forms the cutting edge. Figures of between 62 and 65 on the Rockwell C scale are usually quoted. The harder the steel, the more brittle it becomes, explaining why they are of laminated construction. The thin, hard layer of cutting steel is forge-welded to a soft body and shank. On high-quality chisels, this is old wrought iron, while on cheaper grades it is mild steel.

I understand it's impossible to make a solid, cast-steel chisel of this degree of hardness as it would be too brittle to use. The soft body of the Japanese chisel acts as a shock absorber, allowing the use of extremely hard cutting edges.

# Alloy steels

The modern world has a plethora of sophisticated alloy steels. I have some solid, high-speed, steel Japanese chisels which are great for rough work. Hard and tough, they stand up to considerable abuse, but don't sharpen to a particularly fine edge. This is where the cryogenically treated A2 alloy comes in – it's a tough alloy that can be hardened to Rockwell 62 without becoming too brittle. The edge-holding properties are excellent and outlast carbon steel by approximately a factor of four. The material is capable of taking a fine edge with conventional sharpening systems.

If a chisel edge is chipping, a microbevel can be honed at a steeper angle – 0.005in may be enough

**Improving a chisel edge**

# Grinding and shaping

Whatever chisel you choose to buy, the quality of the grinding and shaping are of great importance. Avoid a chisel with a 'belly' like the plague. This is where the back of the chisel is not straight in its length and has a belly, or a convex bump in the length of the flat side. When a chisel cuts, the path of the edge is jigged from the flat back of the blade. Chisels such as this cannot cut a flat surface without being lifted and control of the cut will be lost.

**Top: An HSS tough site chisel can take a lot of abuse!**

**Below: My new plane blade – a fine example of a top maker's work.**

# Old chisels

Make sure you check the backs of old chisels carefully. A chisel which has been sharpened for years on a hollow oilstone will have acquired a belly from this poor technique. See page 89 for techniques on how to avoid this.

If your stones are flat, it will also be impossible to polish away the wire edge formed when you hone the bevel. New European-style chisels with a 'belly' should be returned to the manufacturer immediately, as attempting to remove significant amounts of hard steel is ridiculously time-consuming.

We can tolerate slight inaccuracies in a Japanese chisel, as the hollow-ground backs mean there is less metal to be removed. I do my primary flattening on an 800grit waterstone, and flatten the stone after about four minutes of work. The general grinding finish of Japanese chisels is very variable, but tends to improve with price. The best shape for the back of a new European-style chisel is a slight hollow in the length of the back, perhaps a few thousandths of an inch. This helps to achieve a well-flattened and polished area adjacent to the cutting edge.

**Below: A poorly ground and shaped chisel, and a better-quality dovetail shape.**

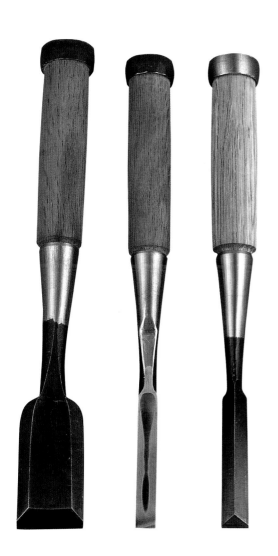

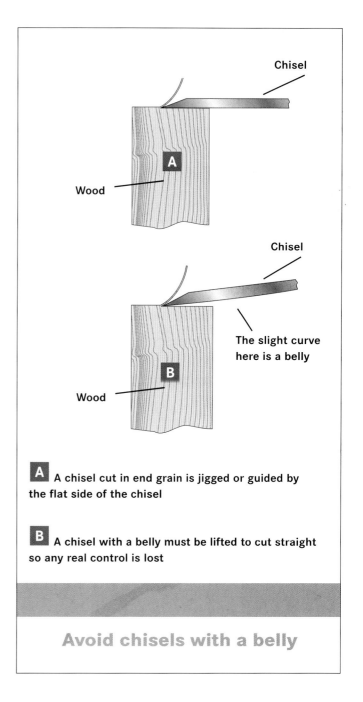

**A** A chisel cut in end grain is jigged or guided by the flat side of the chisel

**B** A chisel with a belly must be lifted to cut straight so any real control is lost

**Avoid chisels with a belly**

# Lie-Nielsen

Thomas Lie-Nielsen has been working on the development of socket chisels for some years, and he has done a great deal of experimenting. He was partly responding to customer demand, but was not interested in producing a chisel unless it was significantly better than those currently available.

The design is based on an old Stanley 750, popular in the USA. I have never seen one in this country, but craftsmen who have originals cherish and value them. The feel and balance in the hand is lovely. The fine edge grinding will be good for dovetail corner cleaning and is maintained throughout the length of the blade.

The steel is cryogenically treated A2, hardened to 60–62 on the Rockwell C scale. This combination should give much better edge holding and should be less brittle than a Japanese chisel. In my limited and subjective workshop tests, edge holding was significantly better than the Japanese chisel I was comparing it with.

## Polished chisels

I don't like highly polished European chisels as too much machine polishing rounds the long edges of the flat back. An edge not sharp at the corners will result if sufficient metal is not removed from the back or the edge. Sharp corners are vital for producing clean corners in joints. The other feature I dislike is the thickness of the edge itself. The bevelling is superficial, and the cross-section approaches that of a firmer chisel. The overly thick edges make cleaning the corners in dovetail work very much harder. Compare these with the thin, nicely ground Ashley Illes chisel.

**Below: An over-polished Two Cherries chisel.**

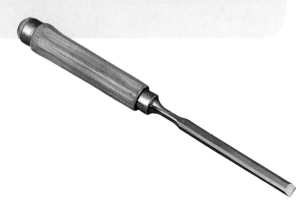

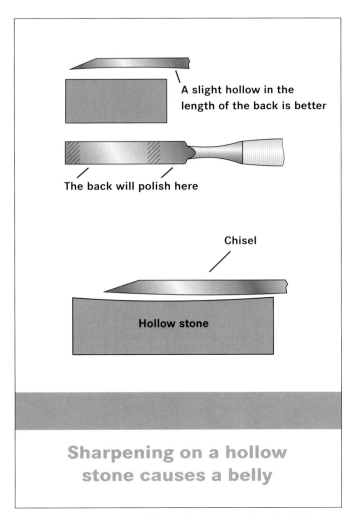

A slight hollow in the length of the back is better

The back will polish here

Chisel

Hollow stone

**Sharpening on a hollow stone causes a belly**

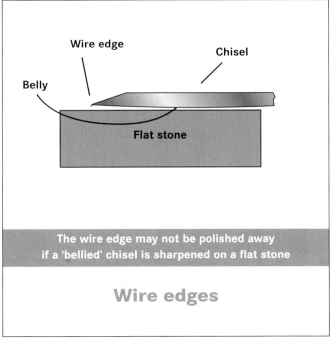

Wire edge

Chisel

Belly

Flat stone

The wire edge may not be polished away if a 'bellied' chisel is sharpened on a flat stone

**Wire edges**

# Handle

The handle is made from well-finished Maine hop-hornbeam, which is tough enough for tapping with a hammer. The socket handle could easily be replaced with a home-turned one, if the shape or size of handle was not to the user's taste. I have used the chisels for some time now, and am delighted with them. Thomas is producing a long handle, at my suggestion, which makes them ideal for paring.

Some of you may infer a bias towards Lie-Nielsen tools, but there are very few manufacturers coming up with new, high-quality hand tools. I predict the new Lie-Nielsen chisels will be extremely popular with discerning users. They should perform extremely well, and will be much more familiar to Western users than the highly strung, thoroughbred, Japanese chisel.

**Top right: The thick edge of Two Cherries and a nicely ground thin edge of an Ashley Illes chisel.**

**Bottom right: The Lie-Nielsen has a fine edge all through the chisel length.**

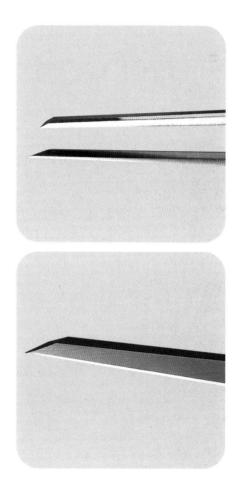

# In Japan

The majority of work in Japan is done with softwoods – so many chisels come ground and honed at 27°. This may explain why many users have problems with edge chipping, when using hardwoods. I hone my striking chisels at 35°, and my long paring chisels at around 30°. However, I am always prepared to adjust these angles for the type of work and the type of timber being used. Morticing in a dense wood might call for angles of 40 or even 45°.

Similar observations apply to Western-style chisels. I am often astonished by the low angles recommended by some American authors – so experiment! If your edges are chipping and breaking down prematurely, try a slightly steeper honing angle, or a microbevel.

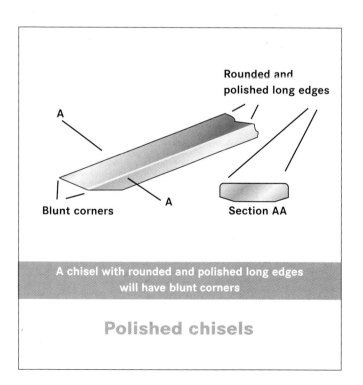

Rounded and polished long edges

Blunt corners

Section AA

A chisel with rounded and polished long edges will have blunt corners

**Polished chisels**

# Sharpening

- Why Grind at All?

- Creating the Ultimate Edge

- Success with Honing Guides

- Using Japanese Waterstones

- Avoiding Hollow Waterstones

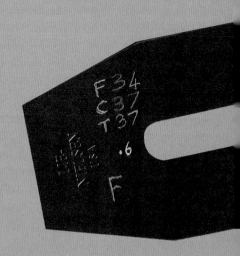

# Why Grind at All?

Rapid and accurate resharpening of chisels and plane blades is the main benefit of taking time and care with grinding and honing angles.

The only reason for grinding bench chisels and plane blades is because it is a quick way to remove metal. We could do our 'grinding' on extra coarse bench stones, belt sanders or even coarse abrasive paper stuck to a flat surface.

I have just watched Harrelson Stanley's sharpening video, which demonstrates the use of Shapton waterstones. He learned traditional freehand sharpening in Japan and never uses a grinder. He demonstrates that a chipped blade can be restored on stones alone. However, he uses a single polished bevel – this has to be the slowest possible method of producing a sharp edge. The single bevel provides the strongest edge but I have found no disadvantages in using a lower grinding angle.

**Below: Showing the use of the Tormek SuperGrind 2000.**

## Benefit

The huge benefit of using low grinding angles is the speed of resharpening and the number of sharpenings that can be completed before it is necessary to return to the grinder. The secret of this method is to keep the primary – 800grit stone – honing bevel as narrow as possible.

By keeping the honing bevel narrow the area of metal in contact with the stone is small and this ensures that metal removal is quick. This is particularly important when creating a slight camber on the edge of a plane blade. When students are struggling with this operation it is always a sign that the primary bevel has become too wide. The wider this bevel the slower and more difficult it becomes to remove metal and change the edge.

The solution for fast shaping is to return to the grinder and reduce the 800grit bevel to a mere sliver. The reason the bevel becomes too wide is because metal is inadvertently honed from the centre of the blade edge, instead of from the outside edges as the curve is being produced. I demonstrate a solution to this problem in my first DVD on plane blade sharpening. The blade is tipped laterally by adding a strip of ¼₄in (0.5mm) plastic to either edge of the waterstone, in turn.

In all sharpening situations, the wider the honing bevel becomes the more strokes on the stone required to remove enough metal to produce a wire edge. The presence of a small wire edge signals that enough metal has been removed to get past the wear and bluntness that use has caused.

There are some interesting microscope pictures on the internet that show that both sides of the tip of a plane blade edge wear in use. I abandoned efforts to touch up a slightly blunt edge on a fine stone years ago because the results were unreliable. Today, I produce a small wire edge on the 800grit stone before increasing the honing angle and polishing the tip on a superfine stone.

  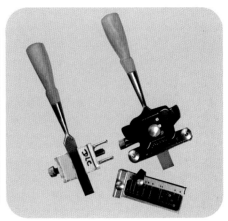

**Top left: The blade with the narrow honing bevel will be much quicker to sharpen than the blade with the wide honing bevel.**

**Top centre: The plastic strip tips the blade and helps to establish a curved edge.**

**Top right: Eclipse-type side clamping guide and the Veritas Mk.11 honing guide.**

**Right: A small sliver of the previous honing bevel is left after regrinding – this contains the shape or squareness of the blade.**

# Angles

I use a total of three angles on my edge tools: a low grinding angle followed by a coarse stone honing angle, which is increased further by 2° when I move to the polishing stone. This is highly unconventional and causes much consternation among some traditionalists. However, the final step of raising the honing angle by 2° is quick and easy to do. If you use an Eclipse-type side clamping guide, the projection is simply reduced slightly, which does not even need measuring. If you are using the new Veritas Mk.11 honing guide, or the earlier version, this angle change is completed by rotating the cam-shaped roller support. This 2° angle change means that we are polishing the business end of the coarse stone bevel rather than the whole surface. When sharpening a chisel this means that I only need to use four gentle strokes on the polishing stone. When I demonstrate sharpening, people are generally astonished by how little time is taken and how few strokes are required.

# Degrees

I am frequently asked about grinding angles and I'm tempted to reply that they really don't matter too much. High precision is not essential in my system and a couple of degrees variation won't have much impact.

The honing angles have greater importance as they generate the edge that cuts. If in doubt you can't go far wrong with the standard recommendation – grind at 25°and hone at 30°. However, there are some modifications to this age-old recipe, which may be of interest, particularly if you use Japanese tools. These almost invariably come with a single bevel at 27°as they are principally used for softwoods in Japan.

I think this is why they have a reputation for chipping when used in hardwoods, though misuse, i.e. levering instead of cutting, also compounds this problem.

One thing that always remains constant in my system is the 2° change when moving from the coarse stone to the superfine polishing stone. I notice that many texts advise honing paring chisels at 25° or lower. However, I also hear a lot of complaints when edges crumble and fail prematurely, a sure sign that the honing angle is too low for the work in hand. My bench plane blades are polished at 35° because I think that the stouter edge holds up slightly better in hardwoods. It is important not to exceed this angle because the clearance angle under the bevel is eventually reduced to the point where the plane will not cut. The advantage of grinding at 23° is that more resharpening will be possible before the primary – 800grit – becomes unacceptably wide and a regrind is necessary.

# Grinding and honing angles for hardwoods

The table summarizes the angles that I commonly use in the workshop, but we should be prepared to modify them according to the type of timber we are using and the type of work undertaken. Clearly the paring of end-grain rosewood calls for a steeper honing angle than that used for soft pine or cedar.

| Tool | Grinding angle | 800grit coarse waterstone | 8000grit polishing waterstone |
|---|---|---|---|
| Japanese paring chisel | 23° | 28° | 30° |
| Japanese striking chisel | 27° | 33° | 35° |
| Japanese mortice chisel | 30° | 38–43° | 40–45° |
| Bench plane blade 45°pitch | 23° | 33° | 35° |
| Low angle block plane blade | 23° | 30° | 32° |
| Shoulder and rebate planes | 23° | 30° | 32° |
| Marking knife | 25° | 33° | 35° |
| Bevel-up bench planes | 25° | Hone and polish at angles which give the Effective Pitch you require | |

**Below left: Truing the Tormek wheel with the diamond dressing tool.**

**Below centre: Two layers of wet and dry reduce the cut when setting the diamond truing device.**

**Below right: Grinding and honing projections marked on a plane blade.**

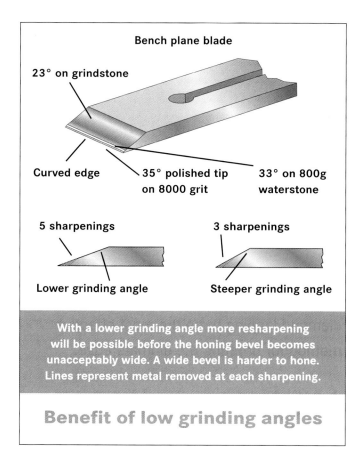

**Bench plane blade**

23° on grindstone

Curved edge

35° polished tip
on 8000 grit

33° on 800g
waterstone

5 sharpenings

Lower grinding angle

3 sharpenings

Steeper grinding angle

With a lower grinding angle more resharpening
will be possible before the honing bevel becomes
unacceptably wide. A wide bevel is harder to hone.
Lines represent metal removed at each sharpening.

**Benefit of low grinding angles**

# Sliver

When regrinding, leave a sliver of the previous honing bevel.
It is important not to remove more metal than necessary when
regrinding a tool.

This sliver contains the 'squareness' of a chisel or the shape of a
cambered plane blade. If we grind right to the edge we will loose
these vital 'shapes' and have to recreate them from scratch, which
is a complete waste of time and effort. We have also shortened
the life of the blade for no reason.

I can only think of two cases where I would grind up to and past
the existing edge. The first would be if a large chip was present.
The second would be to remove a small problem area adjacent
to the edge, when preparing the back of a new chisel or plane
blade – those infuriating corners where the surface falls away
and will not polish. Shortening a new tool by a millimetre or two
is often far quicker than trying to remove sufficient metal off the
whole of the flat back.

**Right: Black felt-tip ink provides feedback
about the squareness of the grind.
The clamping bar needs tilting.**

# Grinder

We have used the large Tormek grinder for many years so 'blued',
overheated blades are not an issue. It is an excellent grinding
machine but I do not entirely agree with the manufacturer's view
that it is a complete sharpening system, preferring to prepare flat
blade backs and hone edges on waterstones. Using the side of the
grinding wheel to remove manufacturers' grinding marks from the
flat side of chisels and plane blades is potentially disastrous, as
one student found to his cost this summer. I also have little use for
the stone grader as I find it impossible to keep the surface of the
stone true. Keeping the surface of the stone parallel to the bar is
vital for repeatable grinding and this is only certain if you purchase
the diamond wheel dressing device.

I set the bar at a standard height from the surface of the stone,
using a piece of 9mm-thick MDF or ply as a gauge. The surface
of the wheel is then lightly 'turned' with the diamond dresser, and
the bar is not moved again until the next dressing is required.

If you constantly adjust the height of the bar it is unlikely to remain
parallel to the surface. When setting the dresser, I introduce two
layers of scrap 240grit wet and dry between the diamond cluster
and the surface of the stone. This provides a lighter cut, removing
less of the surface than the method described on the box.

Keeping the bar at a standard height ensures repeatability,
allowing the same projection from the plane blade jig every
time a regrind is necessary. Having worked out and measured
the projection required, I scribe or engrave this figure on the top
of each plane blade so that the information – and my eclipse
guide honing projections – are readily to hand. Working out the
projection for the first time is a bit of a 'suck it and see' job.
Estimate, grind, measure the resulting angle and adjust the
projection till you achieve the angle you require.

When grinding chisels it is vital to keep the top clamping bar as
parallel as possible to the fixed plate. Subtle adjustments to the
tilt of the top bar will affect the 'squareness' of the grind, so some
trial and error will be called for.

Black felt-tip ink applied to the existing bevel (see above) provides
valuable feedback. It is unfortunate that the flat sides of blades
register against this moving bar, things would be more satisfactory
if this register surface was fixed. I hope that some of these
suggestions will help you with the speed and accuracy of your
sharpening, which must be undertaken at regular intervals. Four
minutes should be sufficient for the pleasure and control of
working with a freshly sharpened tool.

# Creating the Ultimate Edge

In pursuit of a razor-sharp blade, I have found diamond lapping to be the most effective method for creating the ultimate edge.

It is difficult to demonstrate degrees of sharpness on the printed page – much more satisfying to watch hairs jumping off your wrist! – but I hope that this photograph will give you some idea of the sort of amazing results that this method is capable of producing.

To achieve this incredible mirror-like finish, I flattened the blade with Japanese waterstones, then lapped it with industrial diamond grits on home made, oil-soaked, MDF laps. This magical process was taught me by Mike Stein, an American woodworker and friend of Karl Holtey's. I have never seen anything like it before, and I had no need of this method until the introduction of Holtey's S53 powder metallurgy plane blade.

**Left top: Hairs jumping off my wrist.**

**Left bottom: A well-polished blade acts as a perfect mirror.**

## Duo sharp whetstones

David Powell of Diamond Machining Technology Inc. kindly sent me a kit of DMT products to experiment with on the S53 material. The blue and black whetstones, coarse and extra coarse – made short work of the grinding angle on the S53 blade. There is no need to press hard on these plates, the idea is to work gently and let the diamonds do the work.

# What is sharpness?

A sharp edge is found at the meeting point of two flat planes. For many woodworking tools these planes meet at around 30°. The quality of the edge, or 'sharpness' is governed by the quality of the surface finish of the two planes. A perfect surface finish would be a highly polished flat surface with no scratches at all.

I like to view the quality of edges with a 50X pocket microscope. The finer the polish on the two surfaces the straighter and cleaner the cutting edge appears. There are marvellous electron microscope photographs of sharp edges in Leonard Lee's *Complete Guide to Sharpening* (see Further Reading). They compare edges produced with different grit sharpening stones. When a coarser 400grit aluminium oxide oil stone is used, the edge looks like a saw blade.

I hope this explains why I am excited by the mirror polish produced by diamond lapping.

For many years I have been more than satisfied with the edge produced from manmade Japanese waterstones. They cope perfectly well with the new cryogenically treated A2 plane blades from Hock, Holtey and Lie-Nielsen but failed to sharpen the S53 material satisfactorily. When viewed with my pocket microscope the edge was unusually ragged. The blade was also too hard to grind on my Tormek whetstone grinder.

## New tools

Back-flattening of new tools is done fast with the diamond whetstones. I found the red grade quite sufficient and followed up with the green plate for a finer finish. I next honed a secondary bevel on the red plate and moved over to the green to polish it. The flat side of the blade was then returned to the green plate to remove any residual wire edge. There was no doubt that the diamond stones were removing metal from the extremely hard S53 material and much faster than my waterstones, which were having a serious struggle.

## Close inspection

When the edge was viewed with the 50X microscope it still had that familiar ragged appearance. I looked carefully at the surface finish on the flat side of the blade and noticed a number of deeper scratches running through the polished surface. At this magnification the finish did not look as polished as I would wish. I have concluded that the deeper scratches are caused by 'rogue' diamonds, which stand up higher than their neighbours. I also detected high spots at certain places on the edge of the plate. When a tool back was hanging over the edge of the plate I felt a distinct catch from time to time when polishing. I do not know if the finish of the edges of the steel plate or the plating and bonding process were to blame.

It was slightly disappointing to realize that a quick method of producing the perfect edge was still some way off. However, Mike Stein had informed me ages ago that diamond lapping gave the best result.

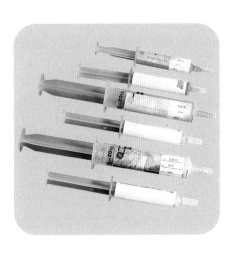

**Left: Diamond paste syringes from DMT and Beta Diamond Products.**

**Right: DMT diamond whetstones.**

# Lapping

Lapping is a well-known engineering technique for producing smooth polished surfaces. The work is rubbed on a plate (or lap), which has been dressed with a suspension of abrasive particles in suitable fluid. The plate is often cast iron, which is softer than the material that is to be flattened. This seems odd at first, but the abrasive grits bed down into the softer material and then proceed to cut the harder workpiece.

# Mike's method

In Mike's method you make your own laps out of oil-soaked MDF. He recommends that ¹³⁄₁₆in (30mm) thick rectangles of ordinary MDF are soaked in Danish oil for 24 hours. The size may be similar to your favourite bench stone, mine are rather small.

Excess oil is removed and the laps are allowed to dry for a month. The working surface is then flattened using well-worn wet and dry paper on a flat surface such as float glass, or a machine table. The wet and dry should be well worn 100 to 180grit. It is essential not to contaminate the lap surface and the idea is that a fingertip is sensitive enough to detect a particle of grit if a loose one should bury itself in the lap surface.

I was impatient to get going, so I glued ⁵⁄₃₂in (4mm) thick MDF to some half quarry tiles with polyurethane glue. When the glue was set I soaked the MDF in Danish oil. The idea was that the thinner MDF would dry a little quicker and the quarry tile would provide rigidity, stability and weight.

When sanding the surface, it helps to judge flatness if you draw a grid of pencil or felt-tip lines on the MDF. You can then see if the grid lines are being removed all at once, which will signal reasonable flatness.

**Above: My laps – ⁵⁄₃₂in (4mm) MDF glued to quarry tiles with polyurethane glue.**

The laps should be labelled, cleaned thoroughly with a vacuum and then stored individually in something like clean zip-lock food bags. They are then ready for use.

# Polishing the flat side

Now we'll look at polishing the flat side with homemade laps and diamond paste. If you have managed to achieve a good finish from fine waterstones or other sharpening media, it may be possible to go straight to 6 or 3 micron lapping paste. All traces of the manufacturer's surface grinding scratches must have been removed from the area near the blade edge. If you are a little dubious about the surface finish, it might be better to start with 9 micron paste.

It may be possible to flatten and polish a brand new blade if you start at the 30 micron level and work down through a series of grit sizes such as 30, 15, 6, 3 and ½.

# Grit sizes

Fine polishing requires that we work downwards through a series of ever-decreasing grit sizes. It is vital that the previous scratches are completely removed with the current grit, before moving on to a finer grit. It is therefore useful to have some idea what grit size your sharpening stones are. This will give you some data from which to decide where to start the diamond lapping. The coarser the diamond grit the more expensive it is.

| Oilstones | Ceramic stones | Japanese waterstones | DMT diamond whetstones | Grit size in microns |
|---|---|---|---|---|
| | | | Black extra coarse | 60.00 |
| Fine India | | | Blue coarse | 45.00 |
| | | | Red fine | 25.00 |
| Soft Arkansas | | | | 20.00 |
| Hard white | Medium | 1000grit | | 15.00 |
| Arkansas | | | | |
| Hard black | | | | |
| Arkansas | | | Green Extra fine | 9.00 |
| | | 4000grit | | 6.00 |
| | | | | 5.00 |
| | Extra-fine white | 6000grit | | 3.00 |
| | | 8000grit | | 2.00 |
| | | 10000grit | | 1.00 |
| | | | | 0.50 |

**Please note: These positions are approximate and for guidance only.
I can find no precise data about Japanese and Arkansas stones.**

I think it is worth noting that a paste such as 6 micron probably puts in scratches which are shallower than 6 microns, as some of each individual diamond particle will be bedded down into the lapping plate surface.

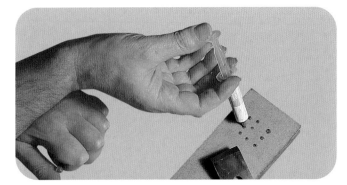

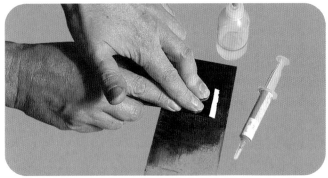

# Using the paste

Apply a few tiny blobs of diamond paste to the surface of the lap. The tool back is placed firmly on top and moved around to spread the paste. It will settle in fairly quickly and begin to 'cut' the metal. As this happens you will see the MDF surface going black. The black is caused by particles of metal which have been removed. Firm pressure is required and when the polishing action gets a bit 'sticky' a small drop of lubrication may be added. I am using 'lamp oil' as a lubricant. This is simply 'less smelly' paraffin sold for domestic lamps. Mike had suggested lamp oil and naphtha but I have been unable to trace naphtha and lamp oil seems to do perfectly well.

A couple of minutes of lapping at each stage with firm pressure seems to be enough. However, one must visually check that all the previous scratches have been completely removed. It helps if one moves the blade so that the current lapping scratches run at right-angles to the previous scratches. It is then easier to see when the underlying ones have been obliterated. The blade is wiped off with a clean paper towel – a drop of oil or acetone may help. You must clean very thoroughly, as contaminating the next finer lap in the series would be counter-productive.

**Left top: Very little diamond paste is needed.**

**Left centre: As polishing continues, surface of lap goes black. Lamp oil used for lubrication.**

**Left bottom: Eclipse honing guide used for bevel lapping. Pull strokes only.**

# The honing bevel

I form this in the normal way, as a microbevel, on waterstones. It takes many strokes to remove very little metal. The red and green DMT plates work very well for this. If the honing bevel is narrow it will be much quicker to polish. I use my Eclipse honing guide as usual and increase the honing angle by a couple of degrees when I move onto the diamond laps to polish. A series of 6, 3 and ½ micron laps will bring the bevel to the same standard of polish. For a plane blade I do the final flat side polish using my 'ruler trick' (described on page 12). In fact the large polished area on the first photo was for demonstration only. On plane blades I only diamond lap the narrow band adjacent to the edge, which results from the 'ruler trick'.

This technique will only interest those who wish to pursue the ultimate edge. I am not suggesting it is an everyday sort of task.

# 'Off the lap'

Spend 50% of the polishing time with the tool edge a little way 'off the lap' to avoid hollowing it. This is the same technique I use for soft Japanese waterstones – a slightly convex surface is infinitely preferable to a concave one. Lapping down to ½ micron produces an incredible polish.

**Below right: The ruler trick gives a narrow band of polish near the edge.**

# Success with Honing Guides

Honing guides are the easiest and most successful way to sharpen chisels and plane blades. Here I explore their uses and a modification to suit Japanese chisels.

I plan to look at the pros and cons of several different makes of honing guide in this chapter. My workshop has quite a collection as they all seem to have their moment. No single type does everything. Razor-sharp edges are the prerequisite of fine work and the easiest way to ensure successful sharpening is to use a honing guide. A guide takes the uncertainty out of bevel side honing, which is the easy part of the process.

In the short course season in my workshop I get my annual insight into the problems amateurs have with sharpening. In the vast majority of cases, it is the flat side preparation and polishing that have gone awry. I described these processes extensively in my first book but it is not possible to convey the whole picture in writing alone. Jim Kingshott, who wrote extensively on sharpening, was a passionate believer in the importance of the student watching the master craftsman and the craftsman watching the student. This centuries-old practice unfortunately disappeared with the demise of the apprenticeship system. Workshop training is the only remaining opportunity.

I think that the scorn heaped upon honing guides is a lingering manifestation of the old protectionist attitude of skilled men – 'Here's how I do it by hand, you are a miserable beginner and in about seven years time you might get a decent result.' Japanese apprentices are made to sharpen single bevels, by hand, for most of the first year of their training. I did not entirely believe this until my visiting Japanese student Kaori confirmed the story. I find this attitude totally unacceptable. My students learn to produce a razor edge on day one, with a honing guide. Leonard Lee is also a strong advocate of them in his excellent book, *The Complete Guide to Sharpening* (see Further Reading).

**Above top: David's collection of honing guides.**

**Above: Holding a skew chisel in the Lee Valley guide.**

# Efficiency of honing guides

Honing guides are more efficient for a number of reasons:

• You can set the required angles precisely to minimize the amount of metal removed. This cuts the time of honing to the minimum and prolongs the life of the tool. The few seconds taken to fix the tool in the guide are more than compensated for by the reduction in honing time. It takes me about four minutes to resharpen, including hand washing, oiling the tool and tidying up.

• Repeatability is guaranteed, provided you note the projections used to hone the angles you like.

• Some say that the roller of a honing guide is going to wear a groove in the surface of the stone. I don't know where this 'old wives' tale' comes from but I have not found it to be true. It is surely the action of the tool steel on the stone that wears a hollow.

• Wide roller, narrow roller, barrel-shaped roller, training wheels and even a ball. These are the variations of rolling support found on my collection of guides. I think it is important to consider the function of each type. We will also see that the tool clamping system is of great importance.

Wide rollers dictate to the user. The edge honed should be straight as the wide roller is stable on the stone, but the squareness of the edge will depend entirely on the positioning of the tool in the clamping system of the guide. Two considerations to watch out for are:

**A** Is the chisel side at 90° to the roller axis when viewed from above?

**B** Is the flat side of the blade parallel to the roller axis when viewed from the front/back?

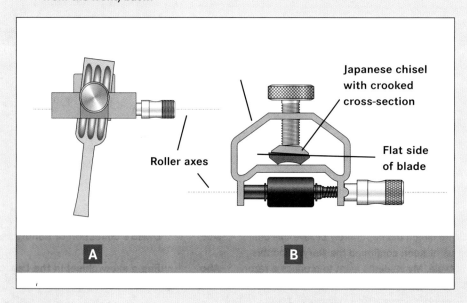

Roller axes

Japanese chisel with crooked cross-section

Flat side of blade

**A**     **B**

# Wide rollers

The Veritas guide has a single, central, screw-operated clamp, which does not hold a narrow chisel very firmly. It works slightly better for wider chisels and plane blades. We can manipulate the 'viewed from above' squareness but will have very little control over the 'parallel to the wheel-axis' position. We should not have a problem with plane blades, but many chisels do not have their blades ground to a parallel cross-section. The surface of the chisel that sits on the fixed part of the guide is frequently not parallel to the flat side. This is particularly true of Japanese chisels.

When faced with a crooked chisel the 'viewed from above' squareness will have to be offset to compensate for the 'crooked cross-section'. This is a compound angle problem which is not easy to visualize. It is similar to the 'Azimuth error', which is found in fixed-bed planes. The bed supporting the blade is twisted relative to the sole of the plane. This requires us to hone the blade of the plane out of square to compensate for the twist of the bed. This issue commonly manifests itself in block, rebate and shoulder planes. The Axminster wide roller guide has a different clamping system. There is a top bar with two knurled nuts at either end. This is similar to the universal jig for the Tormek grinder and may allow us to tip a crooked chisel until the flat side is parallel to the wheel.

I use these two wide roller jigs infrequently. The correct setting of the tool in the jig is not easy. One job that they do well is the honing of skew chisels and marking knives.

# Microbevel

One clever feature of the Veritas guide is the adjustable roller axis. You hone on a coarse stone and then turn the brass adjustment at the end of the roller. This lifts the tool slightly so that you can hone a microbevel, on a finer stone at a slightly increased angle. My comments about the wide rollers 'dictating to the user' also apply to those guides with 'training wheels' – the Stanley, Richard Kell and General. The General guide suffers from a similar, poor clamping arrangement which registers chisels from the wrong side.

The Stanley has a unique wedging action that does register blades on the correct face. Care is needed when operating the two knurled knobs driving the wedge. Unequal tightening can twist the wedge and the plastic retaining 'buttons' can fall off the screw thread when you undo the tool. It will hold short chisels and has this in common with the Kell guide.

The Richard Kell guide is well made and with the back of a chisel correctly registered it will hone a perfectly square edge on chisels, 1 inch (25mm) wide and less. Unfortunately it will not accept bench plane blades. I was unhappy about its ability to hone Japanese chopping chisel angles of 30° and above in a recent review, but Richard has come up with a solution to this problem. Obtain scrap polycarbonate or acrylic from your local sign shop. Cut a rectangle to suit the size of your sharpening stones and then cut a slot in most of the length about 1in (25mm) wide. This slotted rectangle sits on your stone and gives the effect of larger diameter wheels; they run on the plastic while the honing takes place in the slot.

**Above left: The Stanley guide is good for short chisels.**

**Above right: The versatile Richard Kell guide.**

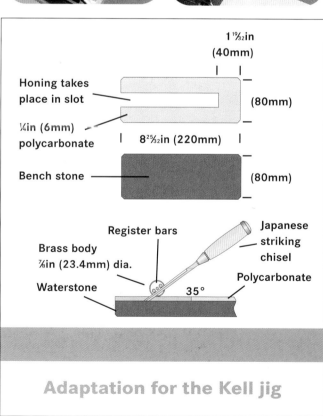

Honing takes place in slot

1 ¹⁹⁄₃₂in (40mm)

(80mm)

¼in (6mm) polycarbonate

8²⁵⁄₃₂in (220mm)

Bench stone

(80mm)

Register bars

Brass body ⅞in (23.4mm) dia.

Japanese striking chisel

Polycarbonate

Waterstone

35°

**Adaptation for the Kell jig**

The Old Record guide No. 161, with single ball is the odd man out here. I have not actually tried to use it yet. The marketing material suggests that you can use the guide to hone in a figure-of-eight motion, thus using a large area of the stone and avoiding wear. I believe the figure-of-eight motion has its proponents, but I cannot begin to get my head round this idea. The possibilities for rounding the edge seem limitless. It might, however, be useful for carving tools.

**Left: Record No. 161 with single ball.**

# Non-standard angles

Determining guide projections for non-standard angles can be tricky. Some of my short-course students are perplexed about how to set a desired angle if the data is not supplied. In the photo, below left, you can see a simple device made with the aid of a plastic protractor. Put the tool in any guide, set the edge of the tool in line with the centre of the radiating lines and squint across the flat side of the tool to see what sort of angle has been set. Trial and error will soon get you to the desired angle. Measure the edge projection from the jig and note it down, for repeatability in the future.

Narrow rollers and barrel-shaped rollers are, in my opinion, infinitely superior. They do not 'dictate to the user', who must now control the honing action with finger-pressure. Speed of metal removal on bench stones is a function of pressure applied to the tool edge. I use one forefinger tip, on each side of a chisel, near to the edge. If the chisel needs squaring up I put more pressure on the side that needs to be shortened. If the edge is square already you need to use even finger pressure on the edges. N.B. When polishing the front of a delicate cutting edge on an 8000 grit stone I use the least pressure possible.

My father's old, red Marples guide has a barrel-shaped roller about ⅝in (16mm) wide. This seems ideal but suffers from the familiar poor clamping screw. I know of no such guide being manufactured

today. The Eclipse and a Far Eastern copy of it have a narrow roller that can easily be overridden by the user. It seems to me that wide rollers are an attempt to de-skill the honing operation.

I have three reasons for wishing to override the roller; the first is to be able to hone a straight but out-of-square edge on a rebate or shoulder-plane blade. As mentioned, this is frequently necessary if the plane has a significant Azimuth error. The second is to be able to hone a square edge on a chisel even if it is twisted in the guide. The third and most important is because I always use slightly curved edges on my bench plane blades.

The blade-clamping mechanism of the Eclipse 36 guide is by far the most rigid and positive for the majority of jobs. It may be tightened gently with a screwdriver and gives a much firmer grip of the tool than the single top screw.

**Below left: My angle-checking device.**

**Below centre: My father's old red Marples guide.**

**Below right: Fingertips control the pressure on each side.**

Chisels are registered correctly from the flat back of the blade – but unfortunately plane blades are not. This means that you need slightly different projections for different thicknesses of plane blade. At 30°, there is a significant difference in projection for a ⁵⁄₃₂in (2mm) thick Stanley blade and a heavy ¹¹⁄₆₄in (4.3mm) thick Lie-Nielsen blade (from the No. 8). For this reason I have taken to scribing my preferred projections directly onto the top surface of my plane blades.

A curved plane blade is relatively easy to produce on a flat stone with a narrow roller. It is much more difficult with a wide roller. This explains why I think that the Eclipse type of guide with the narrow roller is the best and most versatile. N.B. The Far Eastern copy is wide enough for Stanley No. 112 scraper plane blades.

**Above left: Eclipse before modification, front view.**

**Above centre: Eclipse after modification, top view.**

**Above right: Eclipse after modification, Japanese chisel.**

# Japanese style

Some Japanese chisels have a particularly thick blade which makes them difficult to clamp in the chisel grooves of the Eclipse jig. Sometimes I can secure them clamped between the cheeks but not actually in the grooves. You may have to rest mortice chisels on the bars and clamp them between the cheeks of the guide.

The diagram opposite shows a simple modification which I thought up to accommodate Japanese Temple Carpenter's chisels. The guide is disassembled and the top lips of the chisel slots are filed away at an angle of about 83°. Please note that one side has a straight edge and the other a curved edge (when viewed from above). It is worth preserving the given curve as this helps to stabilize chisels that may not be quite parallel in their width. Two plates of mild steel – brass or aluminium, etc. – are then prepared to suit. These plates form new lips to the much deeper chisel-holding space. The plates are clamped in situ and holes drilled and tapped to attach them to the cast alloy body of the guide. I used some 4BA, stainless, countersunk head, model engineering bolts that happened to be handy. The modification is a great success and there is room for most of the large chisels that I have come across so far.

The General off-stone guide has very occasionally had a use for putting low angle bevels on the flat sides of plane blades. I suspect this model is only available in the USA. Tilgear sells a smaller version but it was unfortunately out of stock at the time of writing. I hope these observations will encourage you to benefit from the accuracy and repeatability of honing guides.

**Above right: General off-stone guide being used to hone a 10° bevel on the back of a shooting plane blade.**

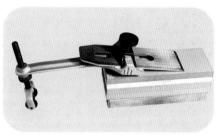

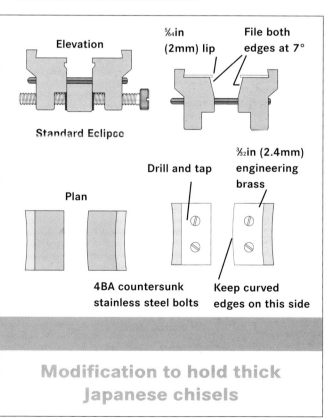

Elevation    ⁵⁄₆₄in (2mm) lip    File both edges at 7°

Standard Eclipse

Plan

Drill and tap    ³⁄₃₂in (2.4mm) engineering brass

4BA countersunk stainless steel bolts    Keep curved edges on this side

**Modification to hold thick Japanese chisels**

# Using Japanese Waterstones

Japanese waterstones offer a cheap, fast and effective way of sharpening tools. Here I will explain how to use and maintain them.

I have used Japanese waterstones for many years because they are low-cost, remove metal quickly and provide a better-quality edge than other materials. They work extremely well on A2 cryo steel and, due to the minute abrasive particle size, provide a significantly finer polish than other systems.

Speed of sharpening is important. I can resharpen a blade in less than four minutes, which includes washing my hands and putting the stones away. This short break from the work in hand should be welcomed – not only does it offer us some thinking time, but also the pleasure of working with a razor-sharp tool when we resume. Struggling with a blunt tool is both tiring and counter-productive. The moment that the faintest suspicion of dulling enters your mind, it is certain that resharpening is necessary, if not overdue.

**Above right: My kit in use.**

## Hollow stones

This rapid breakdown of the surface is both the advantage and the disadvantage of manmade waterstones. I often see with my students' tools that they have not appreciated the speed with which the surface becomes hollow and the damage which this does to the tool. I have developed specific techniques to avoid hollowing the surfaces of my waterstones. In fact, both of the movements described in the next chapter are designed to wear the surface of the stone slightly convex rather than concave.

A hollow or concave sharpening surface which produces a 'belly' or rounding of the flat side of a blade, is very undesirable. It is often found on second-hand tools that have been sharpened for years on hollow oilstones – I also see traces of this loss of flatness on every blade that I have ever seen sharpened by the 'scary sharp' method, which is possibly due to the resilience of the backing. When purchasing old tools it is important to watch out for this fault, which can render a blade virtually useless. The diagram opposite shows how the wire edge on a bellied tool cannot be polished away on a flat stone – it is this polishing away, rather than tearing off by stropping, which is necessary for the finest edge.

# Fast metal removal

The fast-cutting action of waterstones is a result of the rapid breakdown of the surface. Fresh, sharp particles of aluminium oxide grit are constantly being exposed as the friable binding matrix breaks down. This is great for rapid metal removal but it also dictates that we must use a disciplined approach to keeping them flat – I probably do a little flattening about every four minutes of use.

In contrast, a stone with a slightly convex surface tends to promote a minute hollowness in the length of the back of a blade during preparation. This is a positive advantage. When buying new tools I was taught to look for chisels with slight hollow in the length of the back. The advantage of this shape is that the back of the tool adjacent to the cutting edge will be polished quickly when worked on a flat polishing stone.

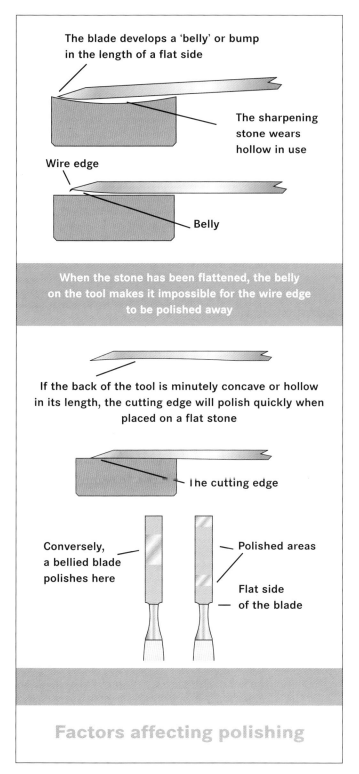

The blade develops a 'belly' or bump in the length of a flat side

The sharpening stone wears hollow in use

Wire edge

Belly

When the stone has been flattened, the belly on the tool makes it impossible for the wire edge to be polished away

If the back of the tool is minutely concave or hollow in its length, the cutting edge will polish quickly when placed on a flat stone

The cutting edge

Conversely, a bellied blade polishes here

Polished areas

Flat side of the blade

Factors affecting polishing

# Affordable

You can do everything with a simple set of three King brand stones, which I will refer to as Coarse 800grit, Medium 1200grit and Polishing stone with Nagura. The Nagura is a small chalky block that is used to work up a slurry on the polishing stones. The coarse and medium stones can be obtained from Tilgear or Axminster Power Tools. I am not very fond of combination stones as the fine side spends time sitting on the bench and risks contamination with stray grit.

If you are on a tight budget I recommend the 6000grit stone for polishing. You will need to buy a separate manmade Nagura, to make up the set.

An 8000grit stone includes its own Nagura. This will provide a fantastic edge and, as the stone has a larger volume than the 6000grit, it will last a long time so it is not as extortionate as it might at first appear. I have recently been experimenting with the 10000grit stone, supplied with Nagura, partly as it is supplied with a nice wooden base. It feels a little different to the 8000grit but does a fine job.

Any of these three polishing stones will give you an edge which is more than adequate for fine cabinet work. Leonard Lee's book, *The Complete Guide to Sharpening (*see Further Reading), shows electron microscope photographs which suggest that the edge from an 8000grit waterstone is slightly better than the edge of a Wilkinson Sword razor blade.

There are many waterstone manufacturers using a variety of different bonding processes. I have certainly not tried them all but we have always had good results from the King brand manmade stones.

Norton have recently produced a set of excellent stones, 220, 1000, 4000 and 8000grit, which I have used and found to be good.

**Above: A set of Norton stones and two Shapton stones with the cast-iron stone lapping device used for flattening the stones.**

# Stone storage

Coarse and medium stones can be stored permanently in water, provided your workshop does not freeze (the expansion of ice will shatter them). I use a couple of seed trays – one for a lid – and add a small dash of bleach to the water to slow down the growth of slimy mould.

The stones can be completely covered, although this is not a necessity. If freezing is a problem the stones only need soaking for about four minutes before use and can be dried out afterwards. Stones of 4000grit and finer are stored dry and not soaked; they are sprayed with a plant mister just before use – Shapton stones will disintegrate into mush if stored in water.

---

**Below left: Showing coarse 800grit and medium 1200grit King stones stored in a seed tray, partially covered.**

**Below right: Superfine polishing stones (8000grit in front, 10000grit behind) with various Naguras and a plant misting spray. This shows a slurry being created with the Nagura.**

# Flattening and bevelling

**New stones will need checking as they are rarely flat. I should no longer be surprised by this sort of thing, but it is a pitfall for the unwary, and the manufacturer or shop is unlikely to convey this vital information.**

For many years I have flattened stones (wet) by rubbing them on wet and dry paper of 180 or 240grit, which is stuck to a piece of float glass with the surface tension of a light mist of water. I stuck my float glass to a piece of scrap Corian, with silicone sealant to make a fixture which drains some of the sludge back into my sink. Sharpening with waterstones is a messy affair, if you do not have access to a sink, although I have managed to work from a couple of buckets at shows. *Sharpening The Complete Guide* by Jim Kingshott (see Further Reading) shows, on page 135, a wonderful teak trough, which holds water. The stones are mounted on teak stands, which hang upside down from ledges on the long sides. I saw this in operation at his workshop and it was most efficient.

Jim used an Extra Coarse Diamond stone to flatten his waterstones and I have recently been advised to try Drywall screen, in place of the wet and dry. This is a 3M product, an open abrasive mesh. It is used to sand down joins in plasterboard. Beware of the stone-flattening devices with deep grooves. Although these appear to be designed for the job, I have had two that were not remotely flat. A concrete breeze block or paving stone would be better.

---

**Below left: My stone-flattening device helps to drain sludge back into the sink. Float glass is stuck to Corian with silicone sealant.**

**Below centre: 3M Drywall screen and coarse diamond plates can also be used for stone flattening.**

**Below right: Drywall screen being used to flatten a stone.**

You can also rub two stones together but this does not necessarily produce a flat surface. It is possible for the two surfaces to be spherical and still fit perfectly.

To be certain with this method, one needs three surfaces to agree with each other. A freshly flattened coarse stone may be used to flatten finer grades, but the coarse stone will not stay flat forever.

I will often rub two stones together, but for a different reason. The surface of a freshly flattened stone can become glazed as the wet and dry paper becomes blunt. This glazing causes the stone to cut slowly at first. Rubbing two flat stones together breaks down the surface a little and allows a stone to cut fast from the first stroke.

# Pencil grid

I draw a grid of lines over the surface of the stone with a pencil to judge the flatness. High spots will be removed first as the stone is rubbed on the wet and dry, while pencil remains in the low spots.

When all the pencil lines have been removed we can assume that the surface is fairly flat. Incidentally, with this method it is possible that you will leave the surface minutely convex, but this will not harm tool backs.

Flattening can be achieved while the stone is either wet or dry. I reshaped some new stones recently with a coarse diamond stone and found it convenient to vacuum up the dust as it was produced.

**Below left: The pencil grid shows us that this new stone is not flat.**

**Below centre: I draw a pencil grid before flattening. Remaining pencil lines indicate low spots in the stone's surface. Flattening is finished when all the pencil lines have been removed.**

# Bevel edges

You will notice pronounced bevels on all the edges of new stones. These should be maintained as the surface is worn down. The sharp edges are capable of cutting you, but if not bevelled they will also crumble due to the softness of binding matrix of the stones.

My sharpening area is a Formica-covered kitchen work surface, next to my sink. I place the stones on a 'sticky rubber mat' to stop them sliding in use. The mat and surface are easy to clean after use. Alternatively you can use simple battens and folding wedges to secure stones, or a rubber-footed non-skid holder, which can be obtained from good tool shops.

In the next chapter I use the preparation of the back of a chisel to illustrate the methods I have devised to avoid wearing hollows into the surface of the stones. The underlying principle is that the edge of the tool is kept off the edge of the stone for 50% of the time. This makes it impossible to hollow the surface, and will in fact produce slight convexity across the width of the stones.

**Below: Maintaining the bevelled edges with coarse wet and dry is important, both to prevent crumbling and to avoid cutting yourself on the sharp square edge.**

**Below right: The sticky rubber mat (from www.dycem.com) is easy to clean. It stops the stones from sliding as long as excess water is kept from getting underneath. Also shown is a non-skid holder.**

# Avoiding Hollow Waterstones

Waterstones wear out quickly. A hollow stone does irreparable damage to the flat back of a chisel. These simple methods avoid this problem.

All new chisels require work on the back or flat side as this surface exhibits coarse manufacturers' grinding marks. Some need less work than others. Honing a highly polished bevel is quick and easy but the edge will not be sharp unless the flat side is equally polished and flat. A sharp edge is found at the meeting point of two flat polished planes. If one surface is covered with deep scratches, the edge will have a saw-toothed appearance under magnification. The electron microscope photographs in *The Complete Guide to Sharpening* by Leonard Lee (see Further Reading) illustrate this point and show that the sharpest edges approach a straight line when viewed under high magnification.

## Chisel

When a chisel is used in a paring cut, the flat side jigs or guides the cut. This is why it is so important to keep the flat side flat. If the back has a belly the chisel has to be lifted a degree or so in order to make a straight cut. At this point the benefit of the guiding surface has been lost and the control of the cut is uncertain.

There is another powerful reason for keeping the flat side flat or even minutely concave. The wire edge formed when we hone a bevel must be polished off on a superfine stone for a truly sharp edge. This is virtually impossible if the tool has any degree of belly; the wire edge will not even touch the surface of the polishing stone.

These are conclusions I have reached after some early difficulties with sharpening. One of the most notable observations is the inconsistency of sharpening. Sometimes we succeed and sometimes we don't.

My current methods produce totally consistent results, which my students are able to replicate after a day or two of practice. The key is in the preparation of a flat or minutely concave back. This is quite impossible if the surface of a waterstone is allowed to wear hollow, which it certainly will if we treat it in the same way as an Arkansas stone. The speed with which a hollow can form is astonishing and the damage done to the back of the tool is significant and difficult to remedy.

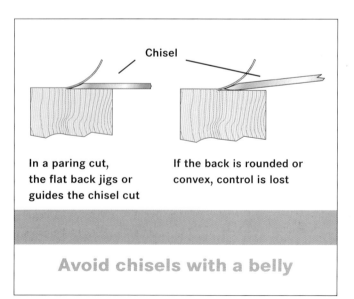

**Chisel**

In a paring cut, the flat back jigs or guides the chisel cut

If the back is rounded or convex, control is lost

**Avoid chisels with a belly**

# Movements

I've developed two movement sequences when preparing the backs of blades to avoid hollowing the surface of stones. The basis is to keep the edge of the blade off the edge of the stone for 50% of the honing time. If this is done it's impossible to wear a hollow in the width of the stone. These movements can be seen on my *Hand Tool Techniques, Part 1: Plane Sharpening* DVD. Chisels ¼in (6mm) wide and under are best prepared with movement two only – there is a danger of causing a belly in the width of the back.

## Movement one

The blade is laid across the stone with its edge about ½in (12mm) off the left-hand edge.

My left thumb applies heavy pressure just behind the grinding bevel, and my right little finger curls gently round the neck of the chisel to stop it pivoting as work begins.

The right-hand thumb and first finger also bear down on the chisel blade to keep it flat on the stone at all times. I do not hold the handle at all as it would be too easy to roll the tool, creating a belly in the width. A full-length stroke is used, to and fro, changing direction close to either end of the stone.

As the chisel is worked up and down the length of the stone, its edge is allowed to 'travel' slowly to the right until it is no more than one-third of the way across the width of the stone. When it has reached this stage it is allowed to 'drift' gently back to its starting point with the edge off the left-hand edge of the stone. The cycle is then repeated. I use about ten strokes 'to and fro' travelling to the right and then drifting back to the left. It is important that the chisel edge spends 50% of its time off the left-hand edge of the stone. This ensures that the stone is worn slightly convex in its width. It is impossible to create a hollow in the width of the stone if you follow this scheme. The left-hand edge will be worn slightly hollow in its length, but we will return to this in a moment. After about 50 'to and fro strokes', the stone is rotated so that the opposite edge is worked.

**Far left: Manufacturer's grinding scratches show clearly next to the finished chisel.**

**Left: The grip used for movement one.**

# Movement one

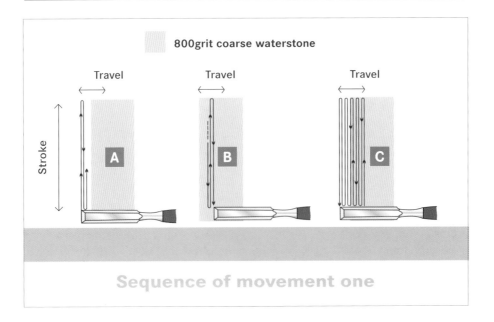

800grit coarse waterstone

Travel    Travel    Travel

Stroke

A    B    C

**Sequence of movement one**

**A** **1** Start flattening the back with the edge of the chisel 'off' the edge of the stone. As you move the blade to and fro (stroke), allow the edge to 'travel' onto the stone

**B** **2** After about ten 'to and fro' strokes, the chisel edge should be about one-third of the way across the stone

**C** **3** After a further ten strokes it should have travelled/drifted back to the starting position

**4** Repeat this cycle

**5** After 50 strokes use the opposite edge of the stone for 50 strokes

**6** Flatten the stone

**Below left: The pencil grid shows the uneven wear of the 800grit stone after movement one.**

**Below right: The grip used for movement two.**

I work at a steady pace, putting as much body weight as possible onto my left thumb. I have seen many students working fast with little downward force. Unfortunately this achieves very little as the rate of metal removal is directly related to the pressure between the tool and the surface of the stone. Wide tools require a large amount of downward force to achieve any significant pressure.

Narrower blades will require less downward force, but the general rule is slow and steady with as much downward force as your thumb allows.

Now it is time to flatten the stone. I mark a grid of pencil lines on the surface and when all trace of this grid has gone, the surface is flat.

If you watch the grid during flattening you will be able to interpret exactly how the surface changes during honing.

You should see the surface worn convex in its width and slightly concave in its length.

This hollow in the length of the edge of the stone could cause a problem with wide chisels and plane blades becoming convex in their width, so on a freshly flattened stone I move on to movement two.

**Left: Chisel back showing crosswise scratches from movement one.**

# Movement two

This is a much shorter stroke across the stone. The chisel edge moves from its starting point, off the edge of the stone, to a point roughly one-third of the way across its width. The 'travel' is a gradual progression down the length of the stone and then back again.

The stone is then rotated and the other edge used before flattening again. This frequent flattening is essential but will not take much work if it is done regularly.

The scratch patterns from these different strokes will be at right-angles to each other. If you watch how the first crosswise scratches are gradually replaced by lengthways scratches you will be able to see if a bump in the width was caused by your first efforts. If a bump in the width is present, movement two is repeated until uniform lengthways scratches cover the back of the blade. If the manufacturer's grinding marks are still visible near the edge of the tool the sequence is repeated, starting with movement one on the freshly flattened stone.

**The arrow shows the length of stroke.**

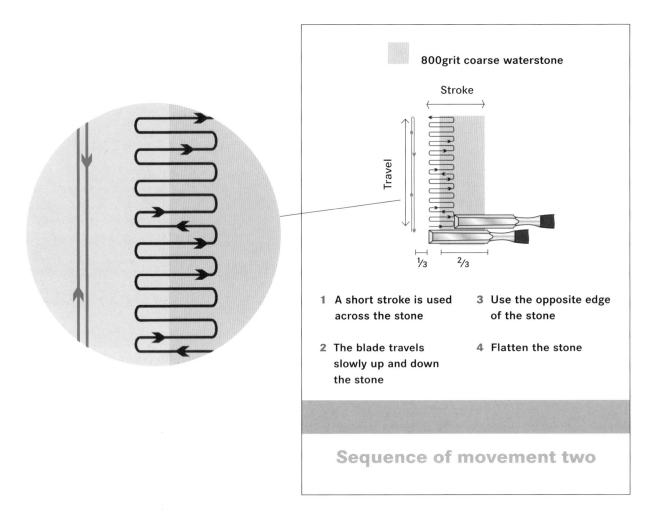

**800grit coarse waterstone**

Stroke

Travel

1/3    2/3

1  **A short stroke is used across the stone**

2  **The blade travels slowly up and down the stone**

3  **Use the opposite edge of the stone**

4  **Flatten the stone**

**Sequence of movement two**

---

Our objective is the complete removal of manufacturers' grinding marks, adjacent to the cutting edge. Even ⅜in (10mm) of well-prepared blade should last you for some years, so I don't attempt to flatten and polish the whole of the back. As the chisel shortens with repeated sharpenings we can repeat the back-flattening process in the future.

According to the quality of the grinding, you may have to repeat the above cycle several times. A badly bellied blade – which should have been rejected at purchase – can take hours, while a well-ground blade might take 15 minutes. You are ready to move to the medium-grit stone when the back has uniform lengthways scratches from the 800grit stone.

## Sequence

I follow with an identical sequence on the 1200grit, medium, stone, starting with movement one and following with movement two, repeating these steps if necessary. This should only take about five minutes as we are only replacing 800grit scratches with 1200grit scratches. The main flattening work was completed on the 800grit stone. I always finish with movement two before moving to a finer stone – this ensures flatness of the width of the back. When satisfied that all traces of the 800grit scratches have disappeared I move to a freshly flattened 8000grit polishing stone.

**Right: This chisel back is twisted and is common problem.**
**Note how the manufacturer's scratches are not being removed from the corner.**

**Left: When uniform lengthways scratches have replaced all trace of manufacturer's grinding marks, near the edge, we are ready to move to the medium-grit stone.**

# Polishing stone

The polishing stone, which could be either 6000, 8000 or 10000grit is prepared with a light spray from a plant mister or drops of water flicked onto the surface with our fingers.

The Nagura, a small chalky block of material, is then used in small circles to work up a little slurry on the surface of the polishing stone. This slurry aids the polishing action. Naguras need flattening from time to time and the sharp edges bevelling, on wet and dry paper, just like our waterstones.

Stones can be easily flattened by rubbing on 180 or 240grit wet and dry paper. The wet and dry is 'stuck' to a flat glass or granite surface with a light spray of water from a plant mister.

The complete removal of a pencil grid, drawn on the stone surface, will indicate when all low spots have been removed. I use movement two only on the polishing stone, remembering to flatten the stone frequently.

We will now benefit from the slight hollow, which will have been created in the length of the flat side of the tool by our previous work. Both movements have a slight hollowing effect on the back of the blade.

This hollow is very slight and might amount to a few thousandths of an inch. You will find that the area of blade adjacent to the edge polishes almost immediately. The other advantage of the slight hollow is that on subsequent sharpenings we have a high degree of certainty that metal will be removed from this critical area, thus polishing away the wire edge.

The idea of a hollow back may upset some purists but I have never found any practical disadvantage. I do not spend a huge amount of time on the polishing stone or worry if the polished area at the tip is not entirely mirror-like.

Movement two – on the polishing stone – is the final step of all future sharpenings, so the quality of polish will improve in time.

I have also noticed that different steels seem to polish differently on waterstones. A2 steel does not become as bright as the carbon steel of Japanese chisels.

However, as long as the scratch pattern is fine and the blade is flat, A2 steel significantly outlasts carbon steel, resulting in less frequent sharpening.

**The Nagura is used to create a slight slurry on the flattened polishing stone.**

# Finishing

- Workshop-friendly Finishing

- Creating a Smooth Surface

- Techniques for a Flawless Finish

# Workshop-friendly Finishing

Finishing can be a major headache for many furniture makers, being one of the most difficult and frustrating tasks we have to do, which is hardly surprising as it is really a specialized profession of its own.

**Above: Carlton House desk in Macassar ebony by Richard Williams. Shellac finish by professional polisher.**

The choice and execution of the finish can enhance or ruin a piece of furniture. I remember a seminar by Martin Grierson where he described spending as long on the finishing as he did on the making. He also felt that a flawless, high-gloss, piano finish was a powerful selling point, as it was something that the customer could not fail to appreciate. I suspect that much of the attention we lavish on our work does go right over the heads of many customers, but perhaps this is our problem and not theirs!

## Multi-approach

Richard Williams has told me that he used a specialist for the French polishing of his magnificent Carlton House writing desk in Macassar ebony. I also know of several workshops that have dedicated spray shops and would not wish to be without them. Much commercial work is sprayed with acid-catalyzed lacquer, although there are moves towards finishes with less toxic solvents these days.

In his book, *Cabinetmaking – the Professional Approach*, Alan Peters describes how he used to vacuum the workshop and spray over the weekend to avoid the day-to-day dust of the workshop environment. Andrew Crawford talks of creeping

stealthily into his tiny workshop, first thing in the morning, so that he can French polish his boxes before much dust is raised.

Sam Maloof wipes varnish and oil mixtures onto his famous chairs, while James Krenov favours ultra-thin shellac to leave the wood looking as natural as possible. For some reason he insists on referring to it as 'polish'. We have used a procedure inspired by his description in *The Fine Art Of Cabinetmaking*, for many years. Our method has evolved and acquired a life of its own so I have no idea whether it still resembles his method at all! Procedures continuously change and develop with experience.

# Back in 1973

When I was beginning my career, a three-coat, two-pack polyurethane finish was in fashion. My preference was for International Yacht Varnish. Some practitioners preferred an infinitely softer, and more user-friendly, one-pack polyurethane such as Ronseal. However, I found these to be rather soft, yellowing and damage prone.

The first coat was thinned for good penetration, while the next two were brushed at full strength. Coats had to be applied on consecutive days or they would not adhere to the previous one. The first two coats had to be rubbed down, with extreme care, to flatten about 60% of the brush marks, eyelashes, dust specks and inevitable runs. Because of the limited drying time the interior of a run was still rather soft and sticky, clogging the wet and dry in seconds. It was difficult to keep a 'live edge' and the handling and support of the components required careful planning and purpose-made stands.

Bristles shed occasionally and had to be picked off, while there was a constant struggle to arrange a suitable light source to monitor the film thickness and avoid bare patches. All this was done while the solvent fume level increased, making you feel unwell! The last coat was rubbed down with particular care, trying to get 85% flatness without cutting through the extremely thin film.

This was then followed by 0000 wire wool to give an even satin matt finish. The wire wool evened out the small percentage of hollows that the fine paper had not yet touched. Finally, it was finished with a thin coat of wax.

The walnut sofa table was finished in this manner and it was a surprisingly successful result. The thin film approach left the pores and grain not entirely filled, resulting in a reasonably natural, woody look. However, I became fed up with the process.

Every major piece had some tiny spot where the film had been rubbed through, exposing the timber. This never showed up properly until the wax was applied, by which time it was too late to repair. These chemically hardening finishes have to be completely removed if repair is needed. It was clear that my brushes and brush skills weren't good enough. I had no suitable, dust-free, temperature and humidity-controlled room in which to operate. Inadequate ventilation of fumes made me feel ill – use an organic fume filter in a mask – and I had not learned the importance of controlling and measuring the viscosity of the varnish.

**Above: My sofa table in English walnut with Indian rosewood crossbanding, boxwood and partridge wood stringing lines and cock beads. Finished with brushed, two-pack polyurethane.**

# Applied films

I would now only consider a brushed finish in very rare circumstances. If a customer is insistent about having a bomb-proof finish, something like Rustin's Plastic Coating, two-pack polyurethane or water-based acrylic might be considered. However, I think it is worth emphasizing that applied films can do only one thing as time passes – they degrade and do not age gracefully! Scratches and chips ruin the surface. If the film is worn away, bare timber is exposed and this gathers dirt.

A good example of this can be seen on the stool rung illustrated overleaf. This was finished with brushed cellulose, a finish that was popular for many years due to its ease of use. An extremely unattractive yellowing has also taken place. The makers switched to an oil finish many years ago and the product is mightily improved. Compare the cellulose finish on the Edward Barnsley chair with the oil finish of one that I made up to complete the set. The original chairs were made around the 1960s and you can see how ungracefully the finish has aged. They will probably have to be stripped and completely refinished.

Above left: Stool rung ageing disgracefully. Brushed cellulose finish.

Above right: Stool rung ageing gracefully. Oiled finish.

Below left: Genuine Barnsley chair, circa 1960s. Cellulose finish showing age and deterioration.

Below right: My copy of Barnsley chair, oiled finish, made 1992.

# Oil finish

A properly executed oil finish is almost entirely in the wood and continues to protect even when the surface is damaged – I'm not referring to a couple of quick coats of Danish oil slapped on at the last moment!

There is a very good description of the process used by Alan Peters in his book, while an even older method can be found in Charles Heyward's *Staining and Polishing*. It is a shame that Alan's splendid work should have been unobtainable for so long. If you do manage to get hold of this book, my advice is to ignore the section on Vaseline finishing. I spoke to Alan one day and asked what work he was doing. 'Stripping and refinishing a piece which had been polished years before with Vaseline,' was his answer. The Vaseline had never hardened and continued to attract dirt like a magnet.

When a dining table with a hand-rubbed oil finish turns up at auction houses, it commands a significant premium. Not many escaped the Victorian obsession for French polishing and their surface appearance is subtle and beautiful.

Above: Oiled bench/table by Clive Lee in wych elm. Hand-rubbed oil finish.

# Charms of shellac

Of course shellac is an applied film of a natural resin obtained from the Lac beetle, but it has many outstanding properties. It will stick to practically anything except wax. It is non-toxic, and even used in some foodstuffs. It has a sweet and pleasant smell, unlike most oil finishes – never use these on interior surfaces – they have a horrible rancid smell when the door/drawer is opened. Lemon oil, which is derived from lemon grass, is one exception.

Shellac can be repaired at will even in small areas, which may be one of the reasons why it is used so extensively by antique restorers. Different grades can be selected to suit the colour of the timber, and the addition of spirit stains and pigments can also be used to manipulate the colour further. But we are now entering the realms of the restorer and I have no intention of trespassing on John Lloyd's territory!

I choose shellac for the interior of cabinets, boxes and drawers. We use it on light timbers where we want to avoid the yellowing and darkening effect of oil. It is also a good choice for any small item that is not subject to excessive wear and tear.

If you are using a wax finish on a timber such as oak, it is wise to apply a few thin coats of shellac before starting. This will seal the timber and prevent dirt from penetrating into the pores of the wood. Wax on bare timber does not seal the wood against grime, which is driven in by further applications.

# Fresh mix

We are having much greater success since we stopped buying proprietary brands of shellac and started mixing a fresh batch for each job. This tip came from an excellent article by Tim Judson in an early issue of *Furniture & Cabinet Making*. Hardness, water resistance and heat resistance are maximized by mixing fresh solutions. These properties decline as the solution ages so we label our jars and do not keep them for more than a month.

I would love to use pure methyl or ethyl alcohol for white timbers as the purple dye in the meths is just faintly discernible – as proved to me by Catherine, one of my students, who mixed her shellac in 'moonshine' brought from Norway. John Curran's approach was to survey the serried ranks of bottles at the superstore and select the palest ones! However, white timbers will alter with age and ultraviolet light as time passes, so perhaps I worry unnecessarily about this detail.

Our mix has evolved to 14g of Liberon special pale flakes in 200cc of methylated spirits. This is much, much thinner than the recommendation on the packet, which is 250g to 1000cc. As it happens, 200cc is a handy volume for small work as it is approximately two-thirds of a jam jar. The flakes are weighed out and the spirit poured over them. If the sealed jar is placed in a warm spot and shaken frequently the flakes should dissolve in less than 24 hours. I have found no need to filter or decant this mixture, as these flakes are de-waxed. If you make up the 'polish' as you approach the final sanding stage, there need be no hold up.

**Below left: My copy of Barnsley chair. Oil finish.**

**Below right: Our very thin mix, 14g of Liberon blond de-waxed shellac flakes with 200cc of meths. The mixture is dated and kept no longer than one month.**

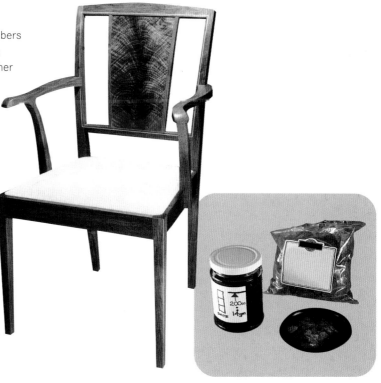

# Creating a Smooth Surface

A flawless timber surface must be achieved prior to applying your finish. Here are some tips for the vital processes of precision sanding and grain raising.

It is fatal to assume that flaws in your surfaces will be disguised by a finish. The reverse is actually true. A finish can highlight and magnify blemishes. The glossier and thicker the finish the worse this will be. This partially explains my obsession with getting the best possible surface from our hand planes and scraper planes. Tear out can be surprisingly deep and difficult to remove by hand sanding.

My sanding routine is usually 240grit wet and dry, followed by 320 and 400grit, minimal to say the least. Its purpose is to flatten the timber surface and remove the planing scallops.

The flattening work is done with 240grit. This may take time and should be rigorously checked. Subsequent grits refine the scratch pattern, each one removing the previous deeper scratches. There is much less work to do with the finer grits. If you cannot get flatness with 240grit, consider using 180 instead.

## Hand-planed surfaces

The surface of a mild hardwood that has been planed with a razor-sharp fine-set plane will exhibit the best possible smoothness, clarity and lustre. However, if your finish requires sanding between coats, we will have a problem with wide surfaces. The sanding block is likely to detect the minute scallops left by the curved plane blade and the finish will be cut through on the high points between the scallops.

This may escape your attention until several coats have been applied. Then long grain, dull streaks appear and are quite impossible to cure without sanding back to bare timber. Even if many coats are built up, the changes in film thickness will still show. Some of my students make this unfortunate discovery almost every year.

I think the concept of applying finish to a hand-planed surface is somewhat academic and not particularly useful. All applied films require sanding, and unless you can find a clever way of doing this with flexible abrasives, sanding for flatness is going to be necessary.

If you are going to sand between coats with a sanding block, relative flatness must be achieved before you start polishing. And the best way to achieve this is by sanding.

It will be helpful to use a larger sanding block to level the surface, as this will flatten the ridges between the scallops. I suggest a smaller sanding block is used for sanding the finish film between coats, as it is less likely to cut through on residual high spots.

**Far left: Stanley No. 80 scraper plane.**

**Left: Lie-Nielsen large scraper plane.**

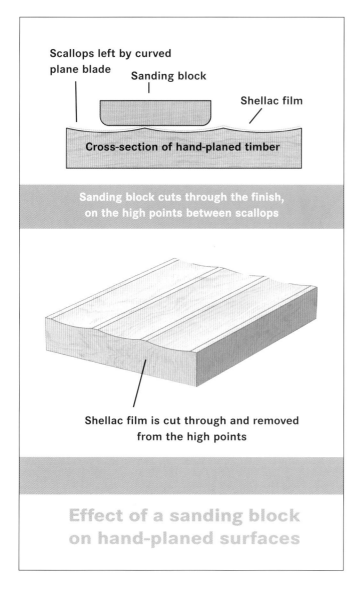

Scallops left by curved plane blade

Sanding block

Shellac film

**Cross-section of hand-planed timber**

**Sanding block cuts through the finish, on the high points between scallops**

**Shellac film is cut through and removed from the high points**

**Effect of a sanding block on hand-planed surfaces**

## Veneered surfaces

It can be particularly difficult to achieve good flatness on a hand-veneered surface. Lumps of glue may remain if the hammering or 'Squeegeeing' of excess glue was not complete. Planing veneered surfaces is extremely risky and not advised; when a plane blade encounters a blister, the loose veneer can be torn away.

Although I have done it, better tools for this work are the Stanley No. 80, or the large scraper plane. The larger the sole the flatter the result. Hand scraping tends to cause hollows, as we inevitably concentrate on the problem areas.

# Making sure the work is clean

I find a vacuum with a soft brush good for cleaning the work. A stiff toothbrush or vegetable brush is good for cleaning the paper. Incidentally, a good bench brush is a valuable tool, particularly good for keeping your work and the bench clean, it will also help to keep the mouth of your plane free from shavings.

One of the dangers of using wet and dry paper is the tendency for small compacted lumps of dust to form. These lumps will burnish and score the surface if not removed religiously.

I do not favour wire or brass brushes as these might contaminate the surface. Any steel particles could cause 'iron stain' problems at the grain-raising stage.

**Far left: Lumps of compacted dust on wet and dry can – and will – damage the surface of the work.**

**Left: A good dusting brush is a valuable tool.**

# Health hazard

Hand sanding is one of the worst sources of fine dust in the workshop. Many timbers can cause allergic reactions, while some are actively toxic. An airstream helmet provides much better protection than a simple dust mask, and my latest precaution is to sand in front of an air-cleaning filter. Our homemade one is an early prototype, which was conceived, made and designed by John Curran.

A good orbital sander followed by a fine random orbit machine will be invaluable on large surfaces, with the huge advantage of built-in dust extraction.

**Right: Sanding while wearing an airstream helmet and using an air-cleaning filter.**

# Sanding blocks

The traditional cork block may be suitable for larger surfaces, such as a panel, but for little else. A cork block can round the edges of a smaller surface, such as an edge, leading to Joyce's 'woolly appearance'. I prefer to call this a lack of crispness or a 'soggy feel'.

Decorative bevels and radiused edges are very difficult to maintain. Bevels should have been left polished from the plane, and we may be better off leaving them alone, rather than risk rounding them with sanding. Delicate radiused edges may call for extra-fine grades of wet and dry.

Most of my blocks are made from ¼, ⅜ or ½in (6, 10 or 12mm) thick MDF – larger ones possibly from ²³⁄₃₂in (18mm) MDF. Bigger blocks, or specially shaped ones, are sometimes faced with cork floor tiles, but the smaller ones generally not. Cork introduces a little desirable resiliance to the surface.

**Above: A laminated curved-face cork-faced sanding block made for a special job.**

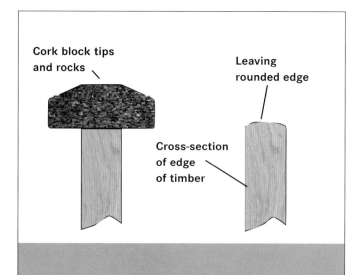

Cork block tips and rocks

Leaving rounded edge

Cross-section of edge of timber

**A cork or wide sanding block will tip and leave a rounded and soggy edge**

# Sanding technique

Sanding is a much-misunderstood topic. Ernest Joyce wrote in *The Technique of Furniture Making*: 'Great care must be taken with hand sanding, which should be regarded as precision work, for the pressure of the hand is inclined to vary with the movement of the stroke, and there is always a temptation to press more heavily over localized defects. At all costs sharp angles and facets must be preserved, or the effect is lost and the work assumes a woolly appearance.'

He also points out that the pressure applied should be firm but light, the stroke should not be too fast, and that the work should constantly be swept clear of dust and loose grit. All these measures are to allow the sharp facets of individual grits to cut the surface rather than to crush and burnish it. If you keep this cutting picture in your mind it will encourage you to change to fresh, sharp paper much more often.

The direction of sanding should always be along the grain; cross-grain scratches are hard to remove and show badly.

Where the work is rectangular, it is often better to use long strokes, which are parallel to the edges of the work. This is also true for complex veneered surfaces; it would be completely impracticable to try to follow the long grain of each section of crossbanding or decoration.

Door frames are a good example of cases where this rule breaks down. I refer to the area where the stile butts against the end grain of the rail. You will find similar problems where flush rails join legs in table construction.

My technique is to select a finer grade of grit than the one you are currently using and sand across the joint at 45˚. This ensures the surfaces are flush and smooth. I now revert to the current, coarser grit, and sand the long grain of the rail to remove the diagonal scratches.

Holding a scrap of wood firmly on the surface, with perhaps a millimetre or two showing, protects the opposing (stile) grain. The stile long grain is now sanded with the protecting block covering almost all the rail grain.

This is the best solution I have been able to come up with. The protecting block helps to minimize the inevitable cross-grain scratches to the smallest possible area adjacent to the joint line.

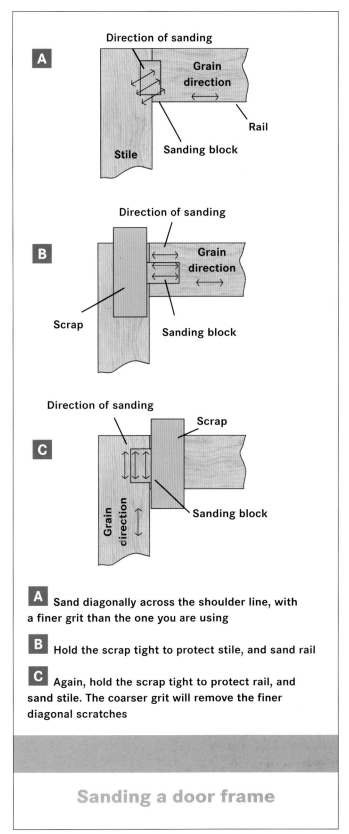

**A** Sand diagonally across the shoulder line, with a finer grit than the one you are using

**B** Hold the scrap tight to protect stile, and sand rail

**C** Again, hold the scrap tight to protect rail, and sand stile. The coarser grit will remove the finer diagonal scratches

**Sanding a door frame**

# Raising the grain

This is a phrase rarely mentioned, except with reference to water staining. I like to do this as a matter of routine, although it is arguable whether it is necessary if solvent-based finishes are used.

When the final grade of sanding is done, the surface is simply damped with clean, hand-hot water applied with a clean cloth and allowed to dry. Now examine the surface with a low raking light. Those fibres that had been compressed and forced into the surface, rather than cleanly cut, will have expanded and are now spoiling the silky feel of the surface. They stick up as fine whiskers which are sanded away with fresh, sharp, fine paper.

I like to raise the grain of end-grain surfaces as well, and it is surprising how rough these can become. The mechanism is different on end grain, but the roughness is equally undesirable. It is also possible that bruises or dents, which were not steamed out before final clean up, are now evident as raised lumps – in fact as 'inverse copies' of their former selves.

I have punched my initials and then planed the surface until they had disappeared. When steamed, the compressed fibres were inflated and rose up in relief. Japanese doll makers are said to employ this technique to form raised tendons for hands.

**Above left: Smooth sanded elm.**

**Above right: Same surface. Showing raised fibres after surface damping, or 'grain raising'.**

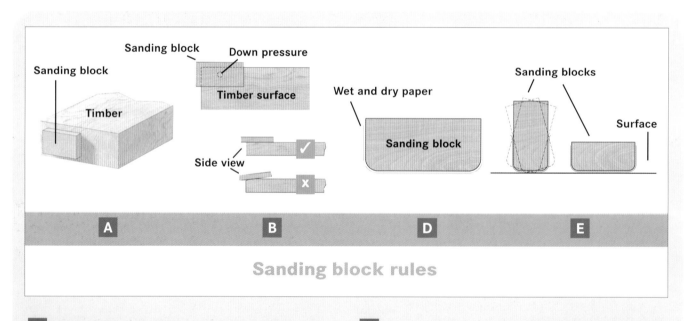

Sanding block rules

**A** The sanding block should always be smaller than the surface it is working on.

**B** The edge of the block should never overhang the edge of the work by more than a few millimetres or the edges will be rounded.

**C** The face of the block must be sanded flat and smooth (see right).

**D** Round or soften the edges of the block where the wet and dry folds around.

**E** Tall blocks encourage rocking, therefore use thin blocks that are wider than they are high.

# Techniques for a Flawless Finish

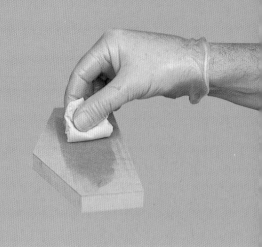

The techniques of steaming dents and bleaching iron stains will assist your preparation before applying shellac and ensure the finish is as good as possible.

We have looked at how to make timber surfaces as flawless as possible before application of finish. However, before proceeding to that final process there are two more potential remedies that deserve to be mentioned: the steaming of dents and the bleaching of iron stains.

**Above: Steaming dents with a domestic iron.**

## Steaming of dents

The steaming of dents is a technique that is not as well known as it should be. No matter how careful we have been in the making process our work seems to attract a surprising number of dents, and I like to steam these before any final planing or sanding. This prevents the possibility of lumps appearing when the grain is raised.

Simply take a hot domestic iron, set for cotton/linen, and touch the tip to several layers of wet clean cotton, above a dent. Maintain the flow of steam for about five seconds – a hissing, steam locomotive-type sound will be heard – and repeat if necessary. The steam will re-inflate the compressed fibres of the dent to a remarkable degree.

There are two distinct types of dent: the smooth rounded type and the sharp angular kind where fibres have been severed across the grain. In the first instance 80–95% success can be expected, while the second will always show because of the severed fibres.

Grain raising and steaming will help to ensure that precious surfaces will not suffer if subjected to damp conditions in the

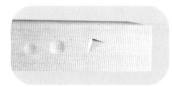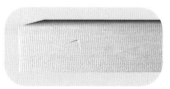

**Above left: Various dents – soft rounded and sharp angular.**

**Above right: After steaming the rounded dents have almost disappeared but the angular, severed fibres still show.**

future. I have heard that gunstock makers have special techniques for de-whiskering their work, using balls of steel wool and blowtorches, but we simply sand the whiskers away, cutting them off with fresh, sharp, fine, paper and a light touch. I sometimes repeat the process once, although I remember a delicate moulding, cut with a blunt router cutter in oak, that needed several treatments. The blunt cutter had severely pounded and burnished the surface rather than cutting it cleanly.

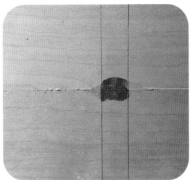

Blue-black 'iron stain' caused by contact with clamp bar.

Oxalic acid solution painted on with non-metallic brush.

The stain is removed by the time the surface is dry.

# Bleaching iron stains

Some people seem to have exceptionally 'rusty' hands, and will leave dark fingerprints over timbers high in tannin. I believe that this is due to uric acid, which is exuded through the skin.

Cotton dusting gloves, available from chemist's shops, may help but if your work has a grubby look, dilute oxalic acid solution – note that it is a poison – will clean it up. The solution can be used for the grain raising, in place of water, and should be followed by washing with clean water, or neutralized with a Borax solution, as residual acid it may interfere with some finishes.

Oxalic acid solution will also remove the blue-black iron stains which are often caused by contact with iron clamps at the gluing stage. Start with a saturated solution, dissolving several teaspoons in half a jam jar of hot – not boiling – water and stirring with a wooden or plastic stick. If no crystals have formed when the mixture has

cooled to room temperature, add more acid. If they have formed then the mixture is saturated. Next, dilute one part solution to three parts of water in another clean jar. Wearing rubber gloves, paint this solution onto the stain with a non-metallic brush or a rag. When done, wash down the whole area with clean water.

# Shellac applicators

Now that the timber surface is as near flat and perfect as it can be made, the shellac can be applied using old white cotton shirts or sheets, the older and more worn out the better; never use synthetic materials.

I fold a 9in (230mm) square several times, so that no frayed edges are exposed. We have also used some wadding from the polish suppliers and made up a covered ball, but whichever you prefer it is important that the working face is smooth and wrinkle free.

These applicators are dipped into the freshly prepared polish and then wiped a few times on some clean scrap wood or MDF. This is to prevent runs or blobs of liquid. The pad must not be too wet, and a degree of judgment is required here. Pads are kept in an airtight container so that the shellac does not harden them.

**Below left: 'Ball' of wadding, covered with cotton for shellac application.**

**Below centre: Simple pad made from an old cotton shirt.**

**Below right: Blotting the applicator on scrap to avoid runs and excessive wetness.**

# Shellac application

It is important to have a suitable light source arranged so that the wetted area of the surface can be seen. A grey sky is one of the best and a high working surface can be helpful. The eye is kept low to view the reflection off the surface, at a very low angle. A bench light or Anglepoise will have to suffice if daylight is not available.

When applying shellac, glide on in the middle and continue smoothly to the end, concentrating on the far long edge first. Next, glide on in the middle with a small overlap and travel smoothly to the opposite end.

The second pass is just the same, ensuring that it slightly overlaps the previous band. Continue like this until the near long edge is covered. It is vital to work swiftly, decisively and accurately. Each subsequent coat softens the previous one, so resist the temptation to mess about with problem areas. Do not try to touch in missed areas until the recent coat has had time to dry.

If the surfaces of your project are worked in rotation, it is likely that the first one will be dry by the time the others are covered. I like to apply three coats before pausing and allowing the shellac to dry for perhaps an hour. This assumes good drying conditions, warm and not too humid. The early coats will dry almost instantaneously, while later coats will take longer.

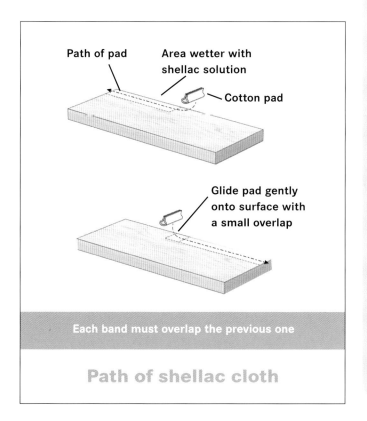

Path of pad — Area wetter with shellac solution — Cotton pad

Glide pad gently onto surface with a small overlap

Each band must overlap the previous one

Path of shellac cloth

# Sanding

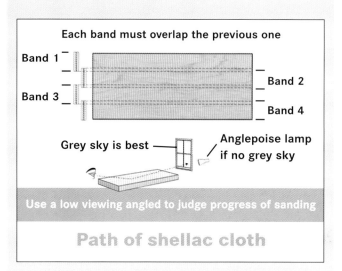

Each band must overlap the previous one

Band 1
Band 2
Band 3
Band 4

Grey sky is best — Anglepoise lamp if no grey sky

Use a low viewing angled to judge progress of sanding

Path of shellac cloth

Having waited for the first 'set of three' to dry, sand lightly with 500grit PSF Longlife open-coat silicon-carbide paper, which has a self-lubricating stearate coating. It is designed for cutting back paint and other finishes and is less likely to clog than wet & dry.

Instant clogging and formation of dust bumps on the paper warn that the polish is not dry enough. It is particularly important to keep the surface of the PSF paper free of dust bumps – I use an old toothbrush or nail brush to scrub them away – or the bumps would leave burnished lines in the surface of the shellac.

It is vital to understand what this sanding is supposed to achieve:
• to remove dust nibs and overlaps of polish
• to remove ridges of polish near edges, perhaps some overspill from when the adjacent edge was coated
• to produce an even scratch pattern on a uniformly flat surface.

The sanded surface should appear matt while the unsanded areas will still be bright and glossy. This difference becomes more apparent as more polish is added. Again, it is essential to find the right viewing angle against a suitable light source as top lighting will reveal nothing.

On early 'sets of coats' aim for approximately 60% of dull matt surface. If you try to get the whole surface evenly matt you are likely to cut through the extremely thin film. This sanding is repeated between each set of three coats.

# How many coats?

For a thin satin matt finish I would normally apply about three sets of three coats. Some people will get away with two sets, while just one set might be sufficient to provide a little dirt protection inside a drawer.

For an unfilled glossy finish I would consider five sets of three to be an absolute minimum.

For a flat, grain-filled glossy finish you will need many more sets of coats and much longer drying times as the film tends to settle into the grain. In fact my method may not be suitable at all.

Experiments and practice are essential for this finishing lark. There was a beautiful brown oak cabinet on stand in the *F&C* competition a few years ago made by Charles Beresford. It appeared to have no finish at all and he told me that he had used very thin shellac. I suspect that his mixture must have been considerably weaker than the one I use.

Having decided the number of sets of coats you are going to use, we should discuss the final treatment of the surface.

# Satin matt finish

Let us assume that you have used three sets of three coats. Please allow plenty of drying time before final sanding – at least overnight and better still several days. Aim at 85-90% of dull matt sanded surface.

The final treatment is to use a pad of 0000 wire wool along the grain, with a firm even pressure. The strands of wire wool should lie at right angles to the long-grain strokes. Wire wool is turned on a lathe, and the strands are triangular in cross section, it is the sharp corners of these triangular strands that do the cutting. The theory is that the flexible pad will dull the remaining 15% or so of untouched bright surface. Dull may not be quite the right word as wire wool leaves a form of satin matt finish – a fancy way of saying uniform wire wool scratches.

Wire wool cutting edges go blunt, so the longer you work with a pad the shinier the surface it leaves. If you have a large table top to do, consider changing to a fresh pad often. The wire wool must be used with great care as it is perfectly capable of cutting through the thin film near edges, or on corners if used too heavily.

Wax can be applied at the end, and the visual results please many people. My personal prejudice against wax is due to its delicate, easily marked, nature.

**Right: Using 0000 wire wool to produce satin matt finish.**

# Gloss finish

If you have built up many more sets of coats and are aiming for a glossy finish, try to achieve a 100% dull matt surface on your final sanding. However, work carefully as cutting through the film is a disaster. Patches that have been cut through are very dull and cannot be made glossy.

One way to test for this disaster is to damp the surface lightly and quickly dry it with kitchen towel. If you have cut through, the wood will absorb water and remain wet and dark while the polish film will dry instantly.

Having sanded the surface flat, first use wire wool and then move on to a burnishing cream like Liberon's which smells extremely similar to Brasso – Professor David Pye mentioned the use of Brasso many years ago. Follow the instructions, rubbing hard with a soft cloth.

My problem with this technique is that some of the scratches caused by the 500grit PSF paper are difficult to remove with the burnishing cream. I feel that I can still see them and that they spoil the appearance of the surface.

**Left: Burnishing cream.**

# Micro-mesh system

I thought I had solved the problem of removing the scratches caused by 500grit PSF paper by substituting Micro-mesh. There is something about the structure of this cloth-backed abrasive which allows the grit particles to roll so that it seems to produce a more even scratch pattern. It also comes in a huge range of superfine grits: 1500, 1800, 2400, 3600, 4000 and 6000.

The grit scale, however, is not the same as that used by UK wet and dry manufacturers, so take care and try some experiments. 1500 Micro-mesh seems to approximate to 400grit wet and dry. The Micro-mesh system is designed to remove scratches from aircraft windscreens and bring them to optical clarity. Their burnishing cream has ultra-fine grit and a special cloth is supplied.

I had decided to use 2400grit Micro-mesh instead of the 500 PSF paper, following this with 3600 and then 4000 grit. On my first small experimental piece the scratch pattern seemed to give a more even satin matt effect than wire wool; however, when I tried to rub down a freshly polished surface, I found that the Micro-mesh was clogging extremely fast. On re-reading the instructions I noticed that it is recommended for acrylic but is less successful on polycarbonate, as the structure of the latter is too soft, so I suspect that my fresh shellac film was still too soft. Maybe if it had been left for a couple of weeks to harden fully I might have had more success. I am sure that Micro-mesh will work well on harder chemical finishes and epoxy.

In the past I have occasionally refined the 500grit PSF surface with wet and dry, working down through a series of finer and finer grits – 600, 800, etc. This has produced good results, though there is still a tendency for these finer grits to clog. When burnished, these gloss surfaces have been much more satisfactory.

**Above: Micro-mesh kit – cloth-backed sheets folded to show both sides with rubber sanding block.**

# Evaluating finish

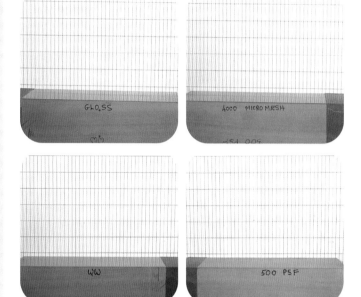

**Above top left: Grid viewed in gloss surface.**

**Above top right: Grid viewed in Micromesh 4000 surface.**

**Above bottom left: Grid viewed in 0000 wire wool surface.**

**Above bottom right: Grid viewed in 500 PSF surface.**

A method of judging the gloss and the flatness of your final surface is shown in Bruce Hoadley's book *Understanding Wood*. A regular grid is drawn on white card, which is placed vertically behind the surface. The reflection of the lines in the surface is then observed at a low viewing angle, the sharpness of the lines being an indication of the degree of the gloss achieved. Distortion, kinks or waviness in the straight lines indicate a lack of surface flatness.

Please remember that a high gloss will emphasize and magnify any surface faults, so I will continue to advocate the satin matt version for the majority of work.

I find this method of using shellac invaluable in the workshop. It is simple, cheap, quick, relatively easy and requires no special equipment. Stop Press: You can eat it! A recent newspaper article informs me that shellac is E904 in food additive labelling.

# Marking and Measuring

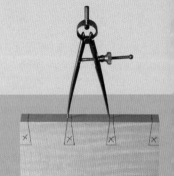

- Precision with a Pencil Gauge

- Marking Out Dovetails

- Face, Edge and Fibre Marks

- Using a Dowel Plate

# Precision with a Pencil Gauge

Turn an ordinary marking gauge into a pencil gauge – a simple but essential tool with many uses.

During the course I run, we spend much time fettling and preparing essential hand tools. The humble pencil gauge has many uses but is often overlooked. It can be used for making repeatable, measured marks on either crude or refined work according to the selection and sharpening method chosen for the pencil. Some prefer to use a ballpoint pen instead.

An example of crude work might be the marking of parallel lines on a roughly planed board so that we can bandsaw components by eye. If you are starting to use a point fence – which is ideal for this job – the presence of a pencil line can be valuable as you will have some visual feedback to warn you if the cut is going astray.

The photograph above shows my much-used gauge and my student's model. You will see that mine has a rather crudely worked recess in the face of the stock, which has room for at least half the pencil diameter. This allows me to mark a line right up to the edge of the timber, which I need to do for the initial marking of stringing lines or small chamfers.

**Above: My gauge and a neater version by my student.**

## Versatile

Pencil gauges have many uses, so it may be worth making two. I use them for marking parallel lines, laying out screw positions, defining saw cuts and decorative bevels. Pencilled lines are useful for inlay work and the precise knife lines can be added once you have established general position with the gauge.

If you wish to find the centre of a piece of wood, you set an approximation and then mark a short line from either edge. It is then easy to split the difference by eye, reset the gauge and home in on the centre without the need for a special (dividing) ruler.

We used a plain beech, square-head marking gauge made by Marples, which is available from Tilgear. The marking pin is simply removed, so that you can start fitting a pencil instead.

**Below left: Short chisel-sharpened pencil for precise work.**

**Below right: Pencil sharpening in situ with a slim knife.**

# Pencil 'tips'

## 1 Experiment

Experiment to find the best hole size for your pencil.
Many are octagonal and made from fairly soft wood. A slightly
undersized hole will compress the edges a little and grip nicely
without you having to bother too much with the locking screw.

## 2 Decide how the pencil is going to lie

Being right-handed and in the habit of pushing my gauges,
I like have it sloping away from me so that it is easier to see the
point, which emerges near to the bottom corner of the stem.
This makes it possible to stop and start lines where you wish.
If the pencil is vertical the point will be hidden under the stem.

## 3 Marking out

With the end of the stem set flush with the surface of the stock
you can trace the edges of the pencil onto the stock. A centre
line can then be marked midway between these lines and taken
over to the top edge of the stock. We will also need a parallel
'guide line' marked about ½in (12mm) away. This line will be
needed later to assist with the setting up in a pillar drill.

---

**Above left: Marking out pencil position including centre
and parallel guide line.**

## 4 Drilling on the edge

Drilling on the edge: we used a machine vice, which should
always be clamped for safety. The stock is tilted at the angle
that you have chosen and the 'guide line' is simply set vertical.
The stem is clamped in position using the yellow plastic
thumbscrew, the end of the stem protruding sufficiently to allow
for the pencil-locking screw. A suitable-sized piece of scrap
wood is prepared and clamped to the face of the stock. This
allows us to start the pencil hole on the top edge of the face of
the stock.

---

**Above centre: Lining up in a drill press.**

The pencil hole is drilled to a depth that just allows the drill to
emerge from the underside of the stem. A larger drill, say one
or two millimetres over the size of the pencil, is then used and
stopped just as the tip starts to enter the top of the stem. The stem
is removed so that this hole may be completed. When the scrap is
unclamped we will be left with a neat half-round channel.

The locking screw needs a clearance hole, tapping hole and
countersink. The clearance hole should stop just over the line
where the saw-cut will be made, but it is best to finish the
screw installation before making the saw-cut (don't forget to
remove the screw before making the cut).

Screw length may be problematical – we need some effective
threads, on the tapping side of the saw-cut to clamp the pencil.
It is better to install a screw that protrudes slightly and shorten
it later, than to use one that is too short. The threads of a
modern chipboard screw are sharper and deeper than those of
a traditional brass slotted screw.

---

**Above right: View of clamping screw and saw-cut.**

## 5 Pencil selection and sharpening

I find an H pencil ideal for precision work on wood, 2H seems
a little too brittle. It is hard enough to wear reasonably slowly
and black enough to be seen. The lead is sharpened with a
slim knife into a shorter version of the chisel shape used for
precision drawing. This makes a delicate 'blade', but one which
does not draw a significantly wider line, as it wears. Other
grades of pencil may suit your applications better – a little
experimenting is worthwhile. Selection of an unsuitable grade
can be frustrating and I would suggest that cheap pencils are
always a false economy.

# Marking Out Dovetails

This technique is an elegant and traditional method for marking out dovetails using a pair of dividers.

I recently learned an elegant 'new' method for marking out dovetails. Of course, it is not new at all, just one of those wonderful old techniques which has managed to escape me for the last 30 years. You may well have seen it in Rob Cosman's excellent dovetailing DVD. I propose to add a few details which are not often mentioned when describing dovetailing.

Rob Cosman learned the method from Alan Peters, who was an apprentice in Edward Barnsley's workshop, so it might be reasonable to assume that it was in general use during the Arts and Crafts period, if not before. Whatever the provenance, I hope you will find it as useful as I do.

Rob demonstrates the technique with two pairs of dividers, but you can use one gauge and one pair of dividers perfectly well. You can mark out any number of components identically, without pausing to construct complex layout lines. This is useful, as the two sides of our drawers must be the same, and you may have several similar drawers in a piece. It works for any number of pins. Another benefit is that virtually no measuring or mathematics is needed. You can see the method on Rob's DVD, *Hand Cut Dovetails*, and you may have seen his incredible demonstrations.

**Above: Paring with chisel skewed slightly, to avoid bruising corners of socket.**

**Below: Homemade dovetail marker with components.**

# Designing joints

When designing through or single lap dovetails, I mark out the 'socket' or dovetail part first. This is not an absolute rule, just my preference. In the drawer-making case this will be the drawer side.

You decide how thick the lap is to be (let's call it L mm). It is important that this is neither too thick nor too thin. If it is much less than ⁵⁄₃₂–³⁄₁₆in (4–5mm) there will be a danger of the dovetails 'ghosting through' the drawer front. Ghosting is a disturbance of the outer surface, caused by the shrinkage of water-based glues as they dry. If the lap is too thick you will just end up diminishing the glue surface area of the sides of the pins. Next you subtract L from the drawer front thickness (DFT). DFT minus L gives the gauge setting for the drawer side-shoulder-line. Use a sharp cutting or disc gauge so that crisp, clean shoulder-lines are cut across the grain. The flat side of the knife or disc must face out from the stock so the bevelled side of the knife is towards the waste areas.

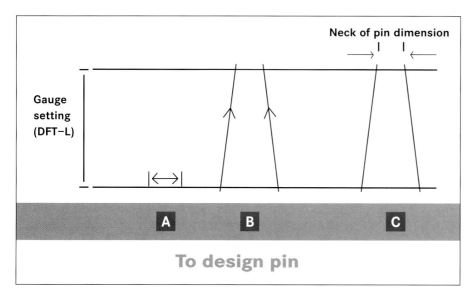

**A** Draw chisel width plus ³⁄₆₄in (1mm)

**B** Project chosen slope lines (for example 1:8)

**C** Measure resulting 'neck of pin' dimension

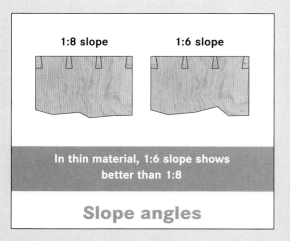

**In thin material, 1:6 slope shows better than 1:8**

## Slope angles

I am not happy with the idea of only one angle for hardwoods and one for softwoods. I think it is more important to design the joint on paper and see what pleases your eye. Timber thickness has a big influence here. If the stuff is very thin, shallow angles appear almost square. I like to use 1:8 for the single lap at the front of a drawer and 1:6 for the thin drawer back, despite the fact that these different angles are both cut in hardwood.

As an aside, it is worth noting that research has been done that proves that extra steep dovetail angles do not increase the strength of the joint. The triangular edges of the dovetails simply shear off along the grain when the joint is broken. Having chosen the width of the 'base' of a pin, I draw in the sloped sides to determine the width of the narrow part of the pin, referred to as the 'neck' of the pin. It is this dimension that will be marked on the end grain of the timber.

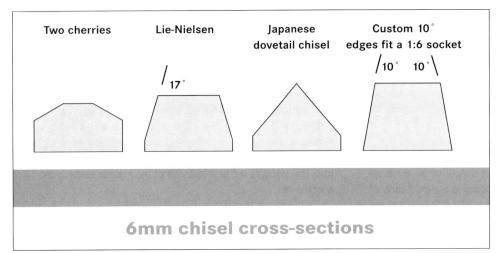

| Two cherries | Lie-Nielsen | Japanese dovetail chisel | Custom 10° edges fit a 1:6 socket |
|---|---|---|---|

17°

10°  10°

**6mm chisel cross-sections**

## Pin size

You need to select a suitable pin size for the job, and I always think it's wise to relate this to available chisel sizes, as nothing is more infuriating than designing a pin slightly narrower than your smallest chisel. In fact, even the best chisels have a small square edge to their cross-section, so it is wise to design the base of the pin about ¾in (1mm) larger than the width of the chosen chisel. This prevents the square edges from bruising the sides of each socket. After you have chopped the shoulder-line, the clearance will allow you to skew the chisel slightly, making it possible to shave the end grain right into the acute corner, without damage.

I do this corner cleaning in horizontal paring mode, with the work held in the vice and before paring is done, I make a release cut. This is one of the best tips for getting a crisp corner.

I have always felt it is highly unlikely that we will have stopped our saw-cut exactly on the shoulder-line. The tip of the chisel just crosses the shoulder-line, and the release cut makes the fibres

stand clear of the side of the socket, or pin, making it much easier to see the lumps which you are paring away (see photograph on page 114). If the socket is too fine for a chisel, a knife or improvised tool can be used to make the release cut.

When the chisel is skewed, the square edge will not damage the sides of the socket. Three-quarters of the chisel edge is supported on the chopped surface.

Many craftsmen grind and hone the edges of a chisel specifically for fine dovetail work. The angle honed would be slightly less than the one chosen for the slope of the pins. Buying a dovetail-shaped Japanese chisel does not guarantee a solution, as most of these still have the regulation square edge.

**Above right: Release cut ensures completely clean corners.**

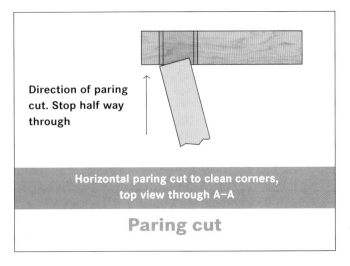

**Direction of paring cut. Stop half way through**

Horizontal paring cut to clean corners, top view through A–A

## Paring cut

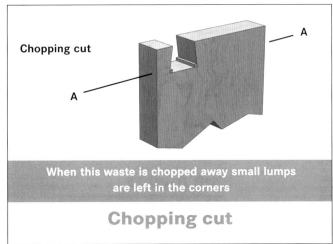

**Chopping cut**

A

A

When this waste is chopped away small lumps are left in the corners

## Chopping cut

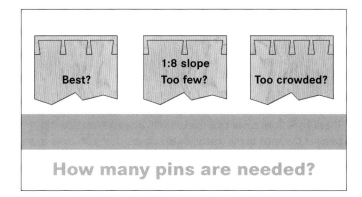

How many pins are needed?

# How many pins?

This decision is not so much a strength issue but more of an aesthetic judgment. Robert Wearing suggests that dovetails should be about two and a half times pin size, but I think we can safely increase this ratio if desired. Too many pins can lead to a crowded appearance, and the decision can be easily made by sketching a few alternative layouts on paper.

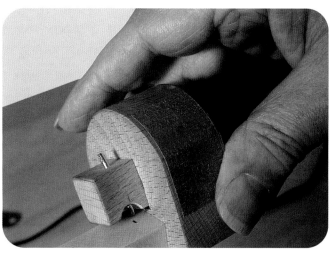

**Right: Marking gauge used to define the half pin position with a stab mark.**

# Half pin width

The name 'half pin' is thoroughly misleading. They need to be strong and whatever size you design, they are likely to get significantly smaller by the time a drawer is cleaned up and fitted. If you use delicate pins, the half pin needs to be considerably wider than 'half a pin'. This vital point is often missed, although it is clearly explained in both *The Technique of Furniture Making* by Ernest Joyce and Robert Wearing's books.

# Material preparation

The components must be accurately prepared. Face/datum sides are always placed to the interior, face edges are usually to the bottom and the ends are planed or shot exactly square and to identical length. It is vital the two drawer sides are an identical, 'mirror-image' pair. Half a degree out of square is not a problem if they are a true pair. A simple shooting board does a great job here, something which is covered in my *Precision Shooting Simplified* DVD. When making drawers please remember to arrange for the outer surface of the sides to plane from front to back so that the drawer front is not split out when planing the drawer to fit.

# Stepping out

Stepping out or marking out is now done on the end grain of the sides with the dividers. One pair is set to the half pin width, although a gauge will do just as well, either by eye or from your drawing. A point is stabbed in from either edge. The second pair of dividers is now set to approximately the width of one dovetail and one pin neck, again from your drawing or by eye.

Starting in one of the stab marks, you step lightly across the width, rotating the dividers by 100° for each step. If the job has two pins you step across three times. The third step must land just outside the half pin stab on the far side. If it does not, make a small adjustment to the dividers and try again. The overlap must equal your neck of pin dimension.

# Marking out

Marking out can now be completed in pencil or pen, on the end grain and outside surface. Knife lines are not necessary, as this is the first part of the joint. If the saw cuts wander a little it will not matter as the pins are traced directly from your sawn dovetails.

# Marking aids

Marking aids will allow you to make the square and sloped line in an almost continuous move. This is much more efficient than the square and adjustable bevel, which I used in the past. The pencil can be felt into the stab marks, the marker is slid up to the pencil and the lines drawn.

The Lie-Nielsen is made beautifully from rosewood and brass. Our workshop-made version was fabricated from Swiss pear and wenge, as we wanted some alternative slope angles, to the 1:6 and 1:7 provided.

The two alloy versions shown in the photograph have an interesting feature: the square slot in the middle, which is useful for marking single lap dovetail pins, near the edge of a board. These knife lines cannot be marked with a square, keeping the bevel of the knife to the waste, as the square cannot be held in a stable position so near to the edge of the work.

**Far left: Marking the square and slope lines with homemade marker.**

**Left centre: Lie-Nielsen dovetail marker, slopes 1:6 and 1:7.**

**Left: Alloy dovetail markers.**

# The overlap

Once the precise setting has been established, you take two steps from each half pin stab, stabbing in sufficiently to leave a mark with each step. I hope some of these observations will help you to improve your results on these fundamental joints. Practice is required but there are many technical issues to consider as well.

**Left: This is what you see after the stab marks from the dividers have been added.**

**Below: Dividers on completed marking out.**

The overlap, or distance from the stab to the final resting place of the dividers, needs to match the width of the neck of the pin we designed. Arranging this may require some trial and error and a few more subtle adjustments of the dividers. Three or four attempts will usually suffice and the process is quick.

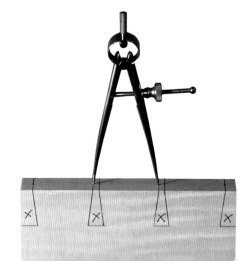

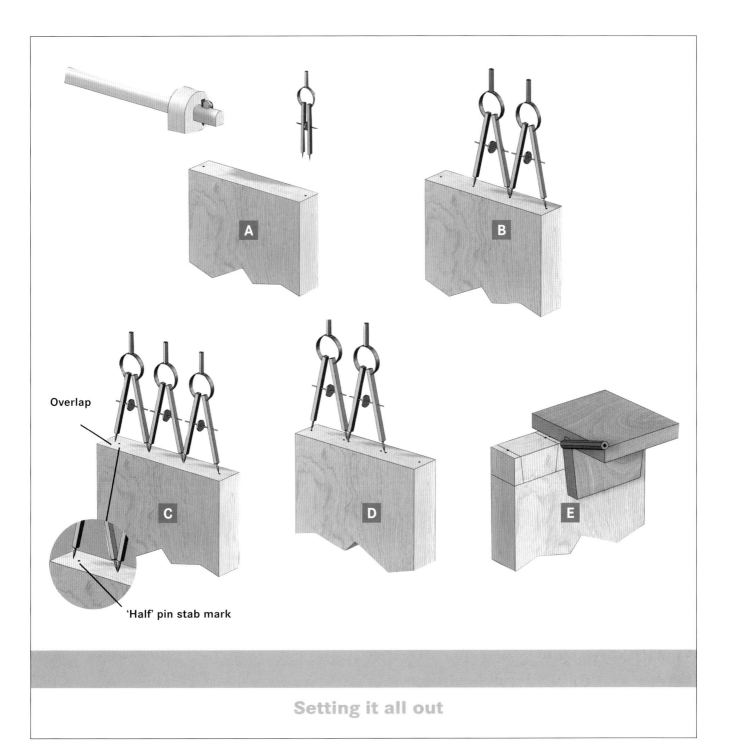

Overlap

'Half' pin stab mark

Setting it all out

A 1 With gauge or dividers, stab in half pin marks

B 2 Set dividers to approximately = one tail and one neck

C 3 Step lightly across leaving no marks – three steps in this example

4 Examine the overlap

5 Adjust dividers and repeat until overlap = neck of pin dimension designed earlier

D 6 Now step twice from each half pin, leaving visible stab marks

E 7 Complete marking with pencil and dovetail marker on end and outside

# Face, Edge and Fibre Marks

This comprehensive set of face, edge and fibre markings will ensure that you are always confident of the correct planing direction.

I do not understand how craftsmen get by with the simple face, side and edge marks which we see in traditional texts (see diagram, below).

In his book, *The Technique of Furniture Making*, Ernest Joyce clearly states: 'When the surface is planed perfectly true and out of wind it should be marked with a "face" mark which should never be omitted from any piece of prepared wood.' He also says: 'Face marks and edge marks must be bold and should be done with a thick, soft pencil.'

It is essential to know where these two datum surfaces are, as they are the surfaces from which all squaring of shoulders, marking of joints and gauging are done. However, the basic marks do not store the planing direction of the surfaces and I consider this to be essential information.

## Mess

Let us suppose that you have completed all the joinery and are almost at the gluing-up stage. Professional makers tend to apply finish to the interior surfaces so that glue squeeze-out (which we try to avoid) can be lifted off without making a mess in the corners. You need a couple of extra-fine sets of shavings and a little sanding to prepare for the finish, which might be thin shellac, wax or spray.

You are working highly figured timber because it is attractive, but it is difficult to plane. Unfortunately, you can't remember which direction you planed it in when preparing the datum surface, so you go the wrong way and create massive tearout. By the time you have rescued the surface, thickness will have been lost and the joints will no longer fit as well as they did when you cut them.

This horror scenario will have you tearing your hair out, and it is the reason why I invented a more comprehensive set of face, edge and fibre markings.

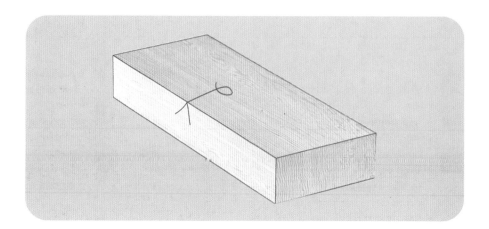

**Right: Traditional marks do not show the planing directions.**

# Inside

**I think it is not generally understood that face sides are always placed to the inside of a carcass, and face edges are positioned on the inside of a frame. The term 'face' has absolutely nothing to do with the surface that 'faces' the public, which will naturally be the most visually pleasing.**

So, the face sides and edges, or datum surfaces, which are chosen early in the job, are usually the least glamorous ones. However, accurate preparation of these surfaces is a prerequisite

for a successful result. You may be familiar with the theory of accumulation of errors. If the groundwork is not right, small errors tend to conspire against us and add up during the job, creating larger errors at the end.

The system of face sides to the inside ensures accurate results, well-fitting joints and nice tight interior shoulder-lines. If I want to judge the quality of a piece, I always look at the internal shoulder-lines. Only the best craftsmen get these really clean and tight, and even the best will have a small gap in a dovetail on a bad day.

# Fibre marks

These are applied while the timber is still in its rough-sawn state, just before going to the machine's planer. I try to determine the majority orientation of the fibres and tubes and mark a pair of lines on both edges of the board to indicate the lie of the wood fibres relative to the surfaces.

This job is much easier with coarse-grained species such as oak, elm and iroko. English and American walnut are not too difficult, but pear and boxwood are practically impossible, as the fibre and tube structure is too fine to see with the eye. In these latter cases, I reach for a thread-counter. This is a type of magnifying glass that was used in stamp collecting and should still be easily available.

In the photograph below you can see the fibre and tube structure quite clearly. A low, raking light casts shadows into the exposed tubes, which appear as dark scratches on the surface.

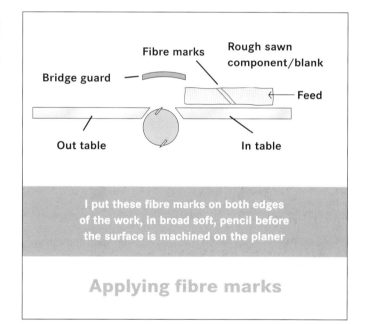

I put these fibre marks on both edges of the work, in broad soft, pencil before the surface is machined on the planer

**Applying fibre marks**

**Above: Brass thread-counter with a small and large magnifying glass.**

**Right: Split tubes showing as dark lines on this edge.**

**Far right: Tubes show clearly through the magnifying glass.**

# Drinking straws

I imagine wood to be like a bundle of drinking straws and the question is, which way can we stroke or plane this bundle so that we smooth down the surface rather than ruffling it up. Another analogy is stroking a cat or dog, with or against the lie of the fur. The stroking down direction is the one we need to plane in, as it will avoid or produce the least tearout.

Wood being an awkward material, the fibres rarely slope up consistently to a surface or edge. They may change direction several times in our board. Ripple or 'fiddleback' timbers give us an extreme example of this phenomenon.

Here, the magnifying glass shows us that the fibre structure goes up and down like a sine wave. Clearly no obvious planing direction here. The other impossible type is interlocked or rowed grain. This is caused by spiral growth which flips to and fro every few years. Very common in African and topical woods, this is typified by quarter-sawn stripy sapele. The fibres in each stripe slope quite steeply in opposite directions. The best policy here is to raise the effective pitch of your hand plane and machine planer blades with a small bevel on the flat side (see page 42 of my first book, details in Further Reading on page 141).

## The fibres of ripple timber are like a sine wave

**Above left: Quarter-sawn iroko showing the dark and light stripes of interlocked grain. The fibres in adjacent stripes slope in opposite directions, reflecting the light differently.**

**Above right: This ash board shows how the changes of colour in the annual growth rings cause the graphic lines on the surface of the timber.**

# Fingertip

I don't like to spend too long deciding, if the fibre direction is not obvious. I either go for the direction suggested by the steepest fibres, which are the ones that would cause the worst tearout, or take a light cut in each direction over the planer. Visual inspection and a sensitive fingertip will immediately tell you which the most

favourable direction is and the edge fibre mark can be changed accordingly. N.B. I always mark both edges with a broad, soft pencil, as we will be removing one set of marks when the machine face edge is planed. The marks on both edges are constantly replaced right through the job, until final finishing.

# Winter growth

A common misunderstanding arises because many people see the ring lines of the timber and assume that the fibre direction will be the same. I can assure readers that occasionally the fibre direction will not be the same as the 'graphic' ring lines, suggest. I can't explain this properly but it is true. This is unfortunate, as the graphic lines, which are caused by colour variation in the growth rings between summer and winter growth, are much easier to see. Many woodworkers look no further when trying to ascertain a planing direction. We see them clearly on the end-grain cross-section, and also where they intersect with the surfaces of our board.

The ash board in the photograph opposite is a splendid example. The pattern produced by these changes of colour on the surface of the board is often referred to as the figure of the wood,

although there are many other contributory factors such as medullary rays, grain and knots. This is a wonderfully vague term, which must have confused generations of woodworkers.

Highly figured wood is simply wood which has a complex growth structure with pleasing colour variations. Nice, clean straight-grained wood, which is structurally desirable, tends to have a very dull figure.

Some tropical hardwoods grow in a uniform manner throughout the year and therefore growth rings cease to be a feature. We are more familiar with temperate hardwoods where the seasons produce clearly defined variations and the growth rings are distinct.

# Face mark

As soon as the face side has been machined I add a face mark, in broad 2B pencil. My mark can be drawn in four distinct ways and it says three things to me: I am a face side, I was planed in this direction and here is the face edge. (You could invent your own mark, I see mine as a pennant or a golf flag. The triangular flag can be seen as an arrow.)

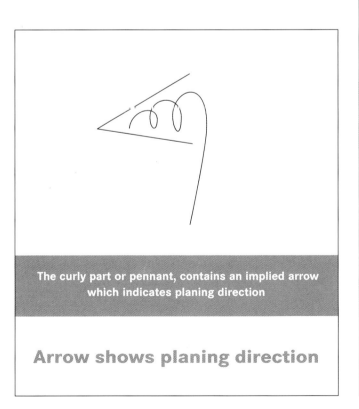

**The curly part or pennant, contains an implied arrow which indicates planing direction**

## Arrow shows planing direction

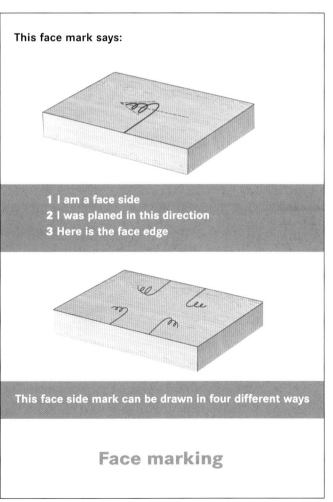

**This face mark says:**

1 I am a face side
2 I was planed in this direction
3 Here is the face edge

**This face side mark can be drawn in four different ways**

## Face marking

I then examine the edges of the face side surface and put on a fibre mark, which indicates my estimation of the planing direction of the edges. This can be drawn right across the face.

If you machine a face edge at this stage you may have to machine against the lie of the fibres, as you do not have a choice of planing direction until the board has been through the thickness planer.

The edge is then marked with its own face mark and the fibre marks are also replaced.

The face mark would indicate the correct planing direction, not necessarily the one we are obliged to use.

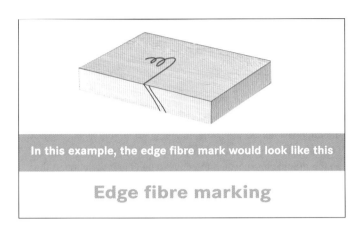

In this example, the edge fibre mark would look like this

## Edge fibre marking

## Complete set

You will see from the photograph below that we now have a complete set of similar marks on both surfaces.

The only time confusion can occur is when the component is square. In this case I make the face side mark large and the face edge mark small!

The beauty of this system is that all the information for the component is stored on each surface. We may well inadvertently plane or machine one set of marks away, but we will never have to make the inspection again as they can be replaced from the information stored on the adjacent surface.

It may become apparent that your first machining decisions and marks need to be changed, when you perfect the face side and edge of each component with a sharp hand plane, but they can be easily rubbed out and redrawn.

## Markings

These markings can be a little confusing to begin with because the face marks tell you which way the surface was planed, while the fibre marks tell you which way to plane the adjacent surface. However, this system will save you immense amounts of preventable work and I cannot recommend it too strongly. As the job progresses, we tend to clean and polish surfaces so you begin to run out of suitable places to put the marks.

We have several cunning strategies, such as making small marks on the surfaces of rebates, or even the bottom of grooves.

In drawer making, where I want to keep the interior surfaces as clean as possible, I might put the face side mark on the outside surface of the drawer sides and front, even though these are not face sides. The face mark has to be reversed, but I am not likely to confuse this machined surface with the interior hand-planed datum surface.

When all else fails the information can be marked on removable sticky labels. It is essential to preserve the planing direction information until the last shaving has been taken, and the final finishing is underway.

It is worth acquiring this discipline and I hope it will help you as much as it helps us.

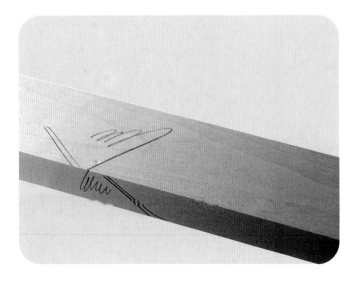

**Left: A complete set of marks on a sycamore blank.**

# Using a Dowel Plate

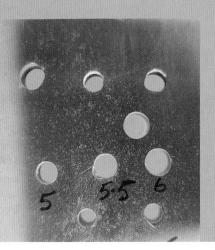

A dowel plate can be used to form hardwood pegs from any timber. This gives you a wider choice of colour for your work.

I wonder how many makers are familiar with a dowel plate? The photograph shows a particularly refined one made by Tom Lie-Nielsen in A2 steel. This is quite the most glamorous one I have ever seen and it is hardened to Rockwell 60-62c. Dowel plates are usually workshop-made, consisting of a piece of iron, obtained from a blacksmith, with drilled holes of various sizes in it.

In use, a roughly sized blank of hardwood is driven through the chosen hole and the sharp top edge of the plate shaves the blank to the exact size of the hole. We thus have the ability to make our own dowels in any suitable hardwood.

**Above: Lie-Nielsen dowel plate.**

**Below: Knocking a blank through a plate with nylon hammer.**

## Technique

It is important for both strength and a clean finish, that the blanks are as straight-grained as possible, and the best way of achieving this is to split or cleave them. They can of course be sawn, but do avoid short or wavy grain. The plate gives best results if the blanks are whittled, planed or turned close to the intended size. The excess is scraped off by the sharp square edge of the plate so the finish is likely to be best when the least is being removed. I think an octagonal section is the minimum requirement.

When making ½in (12mm) diameter ash pegs, for the blind tenons in the back legs of some bench frames, I used a simple V-shaped cradle to plane the blanks close to size. To make the cradle I made a 45° ripping cut on the table saw and then flipped the stock end-for-end, before taking the second cut. Push sticks and guard are essential. I can only do this on my table saw because the riving knife is a fraction lower than the top of the blade and the adjustable top guard is attached to the ceiling above, not mounted on the riving knife.

When the blanks have been rough-shaped it is helpful to taper the end that is going through the plate first. If small, a pencil sharpener might do, if large a chisel, knife or sanding disc will do the job. Clamp the dowel plate above a dog hole in the bench, or screw to a thick piece of timber with suitable, slightly oversized holes drilled. This helps to keep the dowel square as it is knocked through.

Tap the blanks through with a hammer, taking extreme care not to dent the top surface of the plate. The sharp edges of the hole are cutting surfaces and this is why I have shown a nylon mallet being used. Alternatively, knock the last bit through with a slightly smaller dowel. Try to keep the peg square to the plate as you drive it through. Short lengths are easier to drive through. My ½in (12mm) diameter pegs were about 5in (125mm) long. Longer lengths will become more difficult.

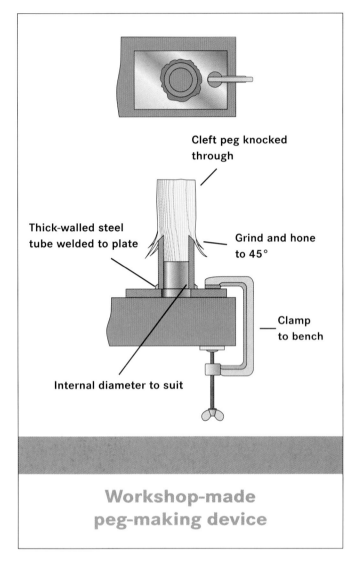

Cleft peg knocked
through

Thick-walled steel
tube welded to plate

Grind and hone
to 45°

Clamp
to bench

Internal diameter to suit

**Workshop-made
peg-making device**

## Perfect size

The finish on the dowel surface is not as good as a turned dowel, but the size is consistent and accurate, time after time. Some authors suggest that the dowels are compressed when passing through the plate, but I haven't found this to be true.

## Benefits

This method opens up unlimited choice of timber. Although some specialists supply hardwood dowel, the most commonly available is ramin. This is a somewhat featureless tropical species, which I believe is under threat. The section is often no longer round as the timber has shrunk or distorted since its manufacture and it may not make a snug fit in the intended hole.

If we make our own, they will fit and we can introduce interesting colour contrast to our designs. I decided to try some harder exotics, such as ebony and rosewood as I had not seen these timbers referred to before. I was delighted to get an acceptable result. Traditionally, oak, ash, maple and walnut were used.

Use dowel plates to check and adjust the size of commercial dowels. My friends Terry and Malcolm of Sawle & Vaughan like to do their dry glue-ups with slightly reduced diameter dowels as it is easier to disassemble the job. They also like to check dowels before a glue-up to see that there is not an oversized one to create havoc during gluing.

## Sharpening

When making your own plate from blacksmith's iron, the top surface is likely to be black and scaly. The drilled hole will not have a sharp edge until this rough surface has been filed and polished to a reasonable finish. This is done with progressively finer grit sharpening or slipstones in the manner used to flatten chisel and plane blade backs. The scary sharp method, using wet and dry paper could be used as an alternative.

I came across another method of quickly producing dowel blanks. I do not know if it would produce a finished dowel. A thick-walled steel tube is bevelled and sharpened on its top edge at about 45°. The tube is welded to a thick plate base, which has an appropriate hole. The plate is clamped and then cleft blanks are driven through the sharpened tube with a mallet.

## My bench frame

Benches I've made recently have had a straight back leg with heavy short rails blind morticed into them. The material is usually iroko – one of the few stable timbers available in 4in (100mm) thickness. In the past I did a glue-up and on removal of the sash clamps one of the joints 'popped' loose. I was unable to determine the cause, as the other joint was well glued. It could have been a badly fitted tenon, or glue failure due to the greasy nature of the iroko. Anyway, the solution was to cramp the frame tightly and install two ½in (12mm) ash pegs.

Here is my method. If a long peg is driven right through it might split out the surface grain on the far side. Pegs driven into blind holes would need substantial saw kerfs in the length of the peg to allow air and excess glue to escape. So the final plan was to drive the long peg most of the way through and insert a short 'dummy' into the far end of the hole. When drilling, I find a sharp lip and spur drill, used in a drill press, gives a clean splinter-free hole. When cleaning up, take care over sawing off and flushing down the protruding dowels. Careless sawing, which marks the surface of the leg, will need much planing to remove the marks. I like to drop a sheet of card (with a hole) over the peg so that we have some warning before the surface is marked.

There is a remarkable Japanese flush-cut saw which has a flexible blade and no set on its teeth. This is flexed slightly, so that the blade is lying on the leg surface while the handle is angled clear. This is a wooden nail saw, Kugihiki Noko Giri, which came from The Japan Woodworker and is also available from Rudolf Dick and Axminster Power Tool Centre. It works on the pull stroke and saws the peg flush, with no marking of the leg surface. If you have not had some practice it is still wise to use a thin sheet of card or paper as protection. My saw came with instructions that the depth of cut should not exceed ⅜in (10mm). It is designed for more delicate pegs. I find that it will saw half way through from either side.

# Results

It is surprisingly difficult to achieve a clean, crisp well-fitting result. Too tight a peg will drag the surface grain of the perimeter of the hole downwards and cause a strange 'halo' effect. Did you remember to try and orientate the growth rings of the peg in a pleasing direction? Sometimes the peg will spiral out of alignment as you drive it in and there is nothing you can do about it.

# Verdict

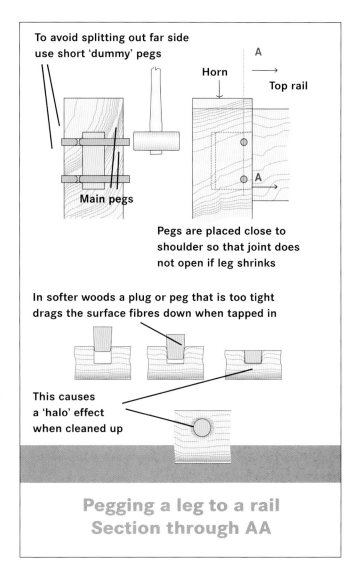

**To avoid splitting out far side use short 'dummy' pegs**

**Horn**

**A**

**Top rail**

**Main pegs**

**Pegs are placed close to shoulder so that joint does not open if leg shrinks**

**In softer woods a plug or peg that is too tight drags the surface fibres down when tapped in**

**This causes a 'halo' effect when cleaned up**

**Pegging a leg to a rail Section through AA**

We saved a great deal of time on the bench frames by using the Lie-Nielsen dowel plate and it worked extremely well. I usually turn the dowels on my lathe and it is a slow process. If you want to make custom pegs the dowel plate is a very useful option.

**Top left: ¼in (6mm) ebony pegs in pau rosa.**

**Top right: Bevelling the peg so that it will not split while being planed.**

**Bottom left: Yew pegs in pau rosa. Note that the growth rings are lined up neatly.**

**Bottom right: Cutting off excess with flush-cut saw.**

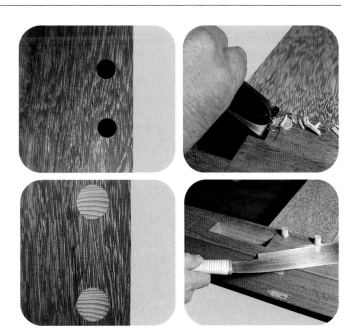

# Techniques in Action

● Table Talk

# Table Talk

This elegant Sheraton-style table shows
how some interesting techniques are put
into practice and problems overcome.

The idea for this table came about from a brief conversation
with a customer. He was an antiques dealer, and he wanted
a display table to store and view small objets d'art. I told him
I was keen on elegant Sheraton-style design, and he said that an
elliptical table would be more unusual than the more common
rectangular type.

I had recently settled into my first workshop, and was keen to
undertake interesting and challenging work. This was clearly
going to fit the bill, but beyond a general feeling that the job
was possible, I really had no idea how much research and
development work was going to be needed. This, of course,

is the classic scenario for losing money on one-off, commissioned
work, as the final product gives no clue to the vast amount of time
which went into solving the many technical and design issues.

**Above: The table, made from Honduras mahogany (legs),
ripple Honduras veneer, Indian rosewood crossbanding and
inlay lines. Interior lined with cotton velvet.**

## Function

I have always noticed that it is easier to sell work that has
a special function, rather than a standard item of domestic
furniture. The world is full of functional or semi-functional chairs
and tables, and it is a rare customer who will spend money for
a particular and personal design.

I exhibited the first of these tables at the Lakeland Guild of
Craftsmen's summer exhibition, and immediately got a second
order. It became a bestseller and nine of these tables were sold
over a number of years. This included a pair to the Dutch
Ambassador in London.

I am going to describe the design and making of this job, as it
contains many interesting techniques and problems, which all had
to be solved.

## The design process

The multiple decisions involved in the design process can seem
impossibly daunting for many beginners. I believe it is a real
mistake to start with a blank sheet of paper and imagine that
you will come up with a masterpiece. Furniture has been made
for thousands of years and attempts to 'reinvent the wheel' are
unlikely to succeed. There may be some gifted people who can
do this after many years of experience, but not many.

My advice to students is to research books, and to try and find
examples of the sort of items they intend to build. It's as useful to
note what you don't like, as what you do. A successful piece can
be concocted from a number of sources: you may like the form of
a particular piece, but not the details, or choice of timber. It is
important to feel excited about your chosen design, but reassuring
to see how other craftsmen have interpreted a similar idea.

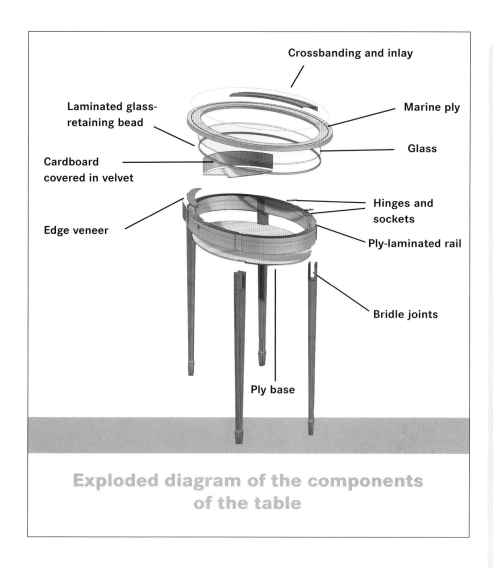

Crossbanding and inlay

Laminated glass-
retaining bead

Marine ply

Glass

Cardboard
covered in velvet

Hinges and
sockets

Edge veneer

Ply-laminated rail

Bridle joints

Ply base

**Exploded diagram of the components
of the table**

# Mistakes?

The inlay lines in the leg have proved unsatisfactory in the long term. I thought it would be a clever feature to make these as fine as possible by deciding to inlay rosewood veneer on edge. This meant the lines were only about ¹⁄₃₂in (0.7mm) wide. Unfortunately, I didn't realize the Indian rosewood (*Dalbergia latifolia*) would fade to nearly the same colour as the solid Honduras mahogany legs.

I hope you will see from the photographs that the lines showed up well when the piece was made, but have now become virtually invisible. This illustrates the powerful design rule, which states: 'If you are going to do something, make sure that it is bold enough to show.'

The other detail I am not sure about today is the gentle radius running down to the top of the spade foot. This gives a 'weak change of direction' relative to the side of the foot.

A design rule for turning and complex furniture mouldings is 'when there is a change of direction, keep it as close to a right angle as possible'. The traditional spade foot has a flat or sloping 'shoulder' which obeys this good advice.

**Below: This table was made to the same design, but in walnut. I include this photograph because the superfine inlay lines in the legs show better, but I felt the figure of the veneer on the rail was rather overpowering and not as subtle as the fiddleback version.**

# Structure

The legs for the table had to be joined to a massive, stable, elliptical rail. They would be bridle jointed into the rail and allowed to protrude from the rail by approximately ⅛in (3.2mm). The inside of the legs would be flush with the rail, so as not to intrude on the interior space, which would eventually be lined with cotton velvet.

The legs would be of conventional tapering form with inlay or stringing lines, and perhaps a spade foot or some other kind of 'ankle' decoration. The rail would also need some form of base, rebated into the underside edge, to provide a surface for the contents to sit on.

**On reflection, the design is something of a mixture, being a Victorian idea, done in Sheraton-style. I don't think there were any oval glass-topped tables in the early eighteenth century.**

The top was effectively a hinged, glazed frame, which would be fitted with a lock. These preliminary ideas seemed eminently feasible, but there were still many decisions to be made. How were the rail and the top to be made?

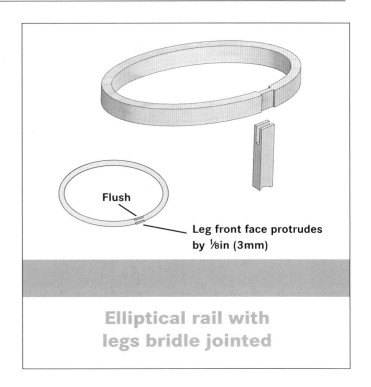

Flush

Leg front face protrudes by ⅛in (3mm)

**Elliptical rail with legs bridle jointed**

# Traditional method

In *The Technique of Furniture Making*, Ernest Joyce suggests that the traditional method of forming such a rail would be to brick-build with softwood bricks, bandsaw and smooth the shape, before veneering or double veneering the exterior surfaces.

However, the damp condition of my workshop made me nervous of pursuing this option: it was a dry-stone walled barn and the wind literally blew through the walls. I had erected an internal polythene tent and attempted to heat the bench area, but it was far from an ideal furniture-making environment. I was almost certain the bricks would shrink and move when the job got to civilization, and that the joins would telegraph, or ghost through the veneers.

The task of smoothing and perfecting the interior walls of the rail also seemed difficult with my limited machinery and hand tools. After some more thought, I decided that it would be possible to laminate layers of ⅛in (3mm) thick birch ply round a former. This would fabricate the inner surface, which would then require little, if any further work. Easing irregularities from the outer surface would not be too difficult.

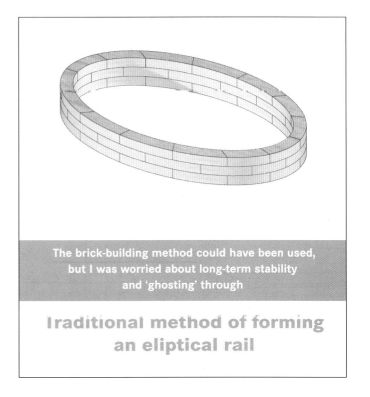

The brick-building method could have been used, but I was worried about long-term stability and 'ghosting' through

**Traditional method of forming an eliptical rail**

# Environment

It also made sense to cut the top from a sheet of marine ply, as this would have no short grain to weaken the rather delicate shape, and would be likely to stay flat in a dryer environment.

These decisions meant that I would end up having to veneer a lot of plywood edges, some narrow and some wide. This was

worrying, as I had been taught that best practice is to lip the edges first, with a tongued strip of hardwood about ⁵⁄₃₂in (4mm) thick. The reason for this advice is that the edges of plywood are 50% end grain, which does not give a good glue joint. There is also a danger of the layers ghosting through as the glue shrinks and the layers move slightly.

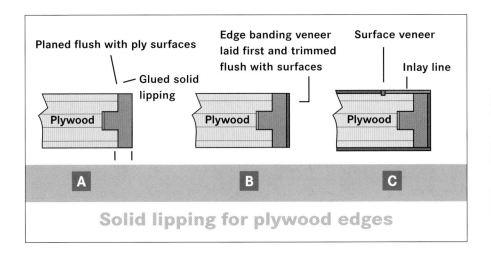

Planed flush with ply surfaces

— Glued solid lipping

Edge banding veneer laid first and trimmed flush with surfaces

Surface veneer

Inlay line

Plywood    Plywood    Plywood

A    B    C

Solid lipping for plywood edges

**A** 'Best practice' solid lipping of plywood edges before veneering

**B** Not more than ⁵⁄₁₆in (4mm) thick to minimize 'ghosting' through

**C** Surface veneers laid last to protect delicate edges of edge banding

# Crossbanding

I was keen on doing my crossbanding with 'gluefilm', as it is less messy and easier to clean up than traditional hot glue (see panel overleaf). This is a thermoplastic, PVA film on paper backing sheet, and is available from Craft Supplies (see page 141). It is worked by softening with a domestic iron, and 'hammering' down the veneer, with a block of hardwood.

I tried some experiments on the edges of ply, and decided that a good joint could be made by using a double layer of gluefilm. It seemed a single layer was too readily absorbed into the end grain. I hoped that the elasticity of the glue line would help to protect against ghosting through. There have been no customer complaints yet, and the first one was made nearly 30 years ago, so it seems that the gluefilm has done a satisfactory job.

**Right: Ironing the paper surface of the gluefilm to tack it to the veneer.**

**Far right: Peeling off the backing paper when the film has cooled.**

**Above top left: Experimenting to see how many seconds of 'dwell' are required to melt the gluefilm.**

**Above top right: Laying the banding after damping surface.**

**Above bottom left: 'Hammering' down the banding.**

**Above bottom right: Trimming the slight overhang flush, with a large chisel and a downward slicing motion.**

I would strongly advise against the use of contact adhesive, as I have seen some beautifully made rosewood veneered work fall apart in as little as ten years. The edge banding is laid with the iron, and 'hammered' down with a smooth block of hard wood, as the narrow edge of a veneer hammer would be too brutal on the non-lubricated surface.

The overhanging edges are sliced carefully off with a large, razor-sharp chisel. The action is a repeated, downward slicing motion, with the chisel held flush to the surface. Everything possible is done to avoid chipping the edges as we slice them off. For this reason the overhang should be kept as small as possible. I cut my banding ⅟₁₆in (1.5mm) over width, so each edge sticks out no more than ⅟₃₂in (0.75mm). Once the edges have been dealt with the surface veneers can be laid.

You may notice, in the photos, that the surface of the marine plywood is unnaturally clean. This is because I had lightly planed the surface, before starting. I found from experience that plywood is not as flat as we could wish, having been mechanically sanded. The planed surface, gave a better bond for the glue, and saved work when the veneers were finally scraped and sanded flat.

# Using gluefilm

The passage below is quoted directly from the catalogue of the Art Veneer Company (now a part of Craft Supplies, see page 141). The company has masses of information on marquetry and veneering, as well as supplies of associated tools and materials:

*'Gluefilm' is a paper-backed roll of thermoplastic adhesive film. It bonds veneer using the heat from a domestic iron. This glue forms a strong waterproof and heat-resisting bond, which withstands temperatures up to 150°F.*

*It can be used on all veneer work except burrs and curls, where there is some risk of the veneers cracking afterwards. The 1m wide material is sold by the metre, and its shelf life is virtually indefinite.'*

The sheet is cut to approximate size and ironed onto the veneer or groundwork with an iron on a low-to-medium setting. Strips of crossbanding can then be cut with a razor sharp knife and a straightedge making sure to keep the grain at right angles to the long edge. I prefer to iron the film onto the banding, as it helps to keep the narrow strips from breaking when cutting. When veneering the edges of plywood I decided to use a double layer of gluefilm as the end grain seemed to absorb too much of the glue.

Square ends can be cut with a large chisel and set square, supporting the delicate strips on a hardwood block. It is relatively easy to judge the vertical squareness of the cut, because of the size of the chisel. The paper backing is then peeled off, after film has cooled, leaving the gluefilm tacked to the veneer.

I decided to do an experiment to find out how many seconds of 'dwell' were needed to melt the gluefilm, at my particular iron (medium) temperature setting. It was worrying not being able to see this crucial change, through the veneer.

I then ironed some crossbanding to a sheet of Perspex. It was possible to see when the glue had melted, so I knew how many seconds of 'dwell' were required. It is best not to overheat the veneer as it dries out, shrinks and ultimately cracks. This tendency can be mitigated, by slightly damping the surface before ironing down. It is odd to have your banding shrinking as you work, and care is needed to avoid open joints. This is exactly the reverse of what we experience with hot hide glue, where everything expands, during the laying process.

# Hinges

It is always wise to resolve hinge matters at the beginning of a job, as problems often become apparent later, when it is too late to make major changes. I found that a satisfactory arrangement could be made by slightly altering a pair of standard strap hinges. This was lucky. Getting special hinges made would have been expensive.

The diagram shows how the line through the centres of the hinge pins can be arranged to just miss the bulge of the ellipse. This means the top overhang acts as a stop for the lid, helping to support it just past vertical, when the table is open. There is not really any discreet space for stays or chains to steady the lid in this job. The protruding knuckle ends of the hinges were neatly inlaid and hidden by the top overhang.

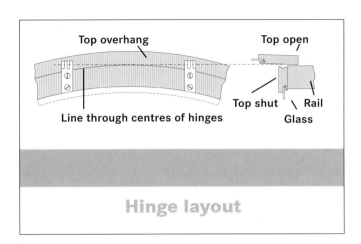

**Hinge layout**

**Right: Standard strap hinges, slightly modified to fit. Also showing cotton velvet lining.**

**Far right: Hinge recess, showing plywood laminations and individual markings on hinges.**

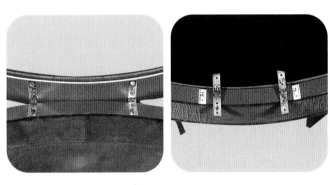

# Lock

**Above left: My escutcheon, an inlaid rectangle of partridge wood.**

**Above right: Small box locks and brass escutcheons.**

I checked in a number of catalogues to find a lock small enough. The important dimension was from top edge to centre of key. I thought the rail would look unsightly if the escutcheon was below centre, and wanted to keep the depth of the table as shallow and delicate as practicable. Eventually I found a small box lock from the Art Veneer Company.

The brass escutcheons available were crudely made, and I did not have much success with my practice fitting. So I decided to use a simple inlay of a rectangle of very hard, partridge wood (*Caesalpina paraguariensis*) which I already had. It is a lovely deep, dark chocolate colour, very fine grained and extremely difficult to work.

At this point I reckoned that the majority of the structural and detail problems had been solved, and it would be possible to make the table. However, the precise dimensions and proportion still needed to be decided and drawn out.

# Legs

The legs on my table are fairly conventional. I would have based them on examples seen in books and friends' houses, but they are slightly more delicate than some I found on a period half-round card table. Having decided that they would be 1⅜in (35mm) square, the thickness of the rail followed as 1¼in (32mm), with the legs protruding from the rail by about ⅛in (3mm).

When I made the first table, Finnish birch ply was ⅛in (3mm) thick. This meant the laminated rail had ten layers of ply. If you build a similar table today, the ply will probably be 5⁄32in thick (4mm) and only require eight layers.

The bottom of the foot is ¾in (20mm) square, and the tapering sides of the leg are drawn to this point. The 'spade' foot, so typical of the Sheraton period, is 'added' to the simple tapering shape. The shape of the foot was decided by drawing variations and deciding which looked best.

The distance of the vertical inlay lines from the edge of the legs was determined by drawing, and small changes were significant. Do consider the top of the leg as well as the foot end. The position of the horizontal lines and the crossbanding width were also decided by drawing different variations. The inlay lines do not line up with the rosewood crossbanding around the sections of the main rail. The depth of the rail had been decided earlier, and had been kept as shallow as possible. This provides enough strength to secure the legs with the bridle joints.

# Ellipse proportion

Mathematical ellipses can be defined by two radii. For any given length there is an infinite range of possible widths. When the two radii are the same we have a circle. I remember having considerable difficulty deciding what width would be appropriate for the length I had selected. Some people are blessed with a particularly acute 'eye'. They know, without hesitation, whether a shape is pleasing to their eye or not. My mother is one of them, and she helped me to home in on the final decision, which was selected by trial and error from repeated drawings.

**Right: My version of a spade foot – weak change of direction and not the best design.**

**Far right: Ellipse drawing device.**

# Accurate ellipses

I used the 'loop of string round two nails' method for sketching the shape. Ernest Joyce calls this the Foci method in the workshop geometry chapter in his book, *The Technique of Furniture Making*. However, I have never managed to get this to work satisfactorily for precise drawing, and realized that I would need a more accurate method for marking out the laminating former and the top. The string always seems to have too much stretch, or not enough flexibility to bend round the nails.

Joyce describes two more drawing methods – the trammel and rectangle. Both are somewhat cumbersome, and do not actually produce a crisp finished line to work to. The trammel method can be successfully adapted to produce a mechanical device which will draw beautiful lines. This is the basis of the Trend ellipse routing jigs and the high precision Microfence version from America.

# Drawing device

A simple version can be made by routing shallow, 5⁄64–⅛in (2–3mm) wide grooves at right angles in a baseboard of MDF. The width needs to closely match the diameter of some straight metal pins, which need to slide freely, without slop, in the grooves. I often use short sections of round nails for the pins. A trammel or wooden bar is then drilled in three places, once at the end to fit a drawing pen or scribe, and twice for a tight fit on the two metal pins which define R1 and R2 (the major and minor radii that define an ellipse).

This set up will draw an excellent line, and can be made in the workshop in a short time. I have seen a much stouter version made by Malcolm Vaughan, which had a router attached to the far end. Instead of pins, he had screws and washers fixing through the trammel into dovetail-shaped sliding blocks, which slid in dovetailed housings. This is an example of how a good craftsman will make a jig, without buying the commercial version.

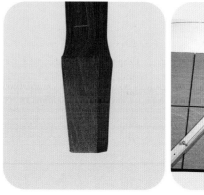

# The top

I described the problems of hinging on page 135, and a ⅝in (16mm) overhang, for a ⅝in (16mm) thick top seemed suitable for this job. The inner edge of the top overhangs the interior by approximately ⁵⁄₁₆in (8mm).

I considered the thickness of the interior lining, and the position of the laminated glazing bead, which holds the glass in place. I did not want to obscure the contents of the display table with a large overhang and the resulting top width was 2in (50mm).

The photograph above shows an arrangement of crossbanding and inlay lines which did not work at all, and I feel the final version is infinitely better. The experimental piece had an unfortunate 'railway track' feel, while the later version seems to lead the eye towards the glass and the contents. The leg positions were also decided by eye and experiment. Having discussed many of the structural and design issues, I will now describe some aspects of the making.

**Above: 'Railway track' sample, not used for the top.**

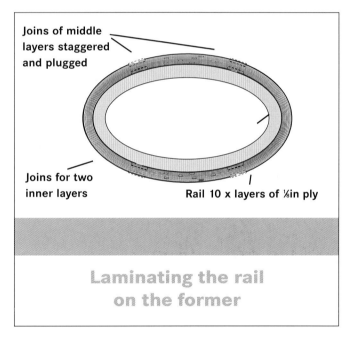

Ply

End-grain softwood

**Ply and softwood former, glued and screwed together. Outside edge faired after glue-up**

## Shaping the former

Joins of middle layers staggered and plugged

Joins for two inner layers

Rail 10 x layers of ⅛in ply

## Laminating the rail on the former

# Shaping the former

I used vertical softwood blocks between two layers of plywood to make the former. The edges of the softwood stuck slightly over the pre-shaped ply bottom layer. This was to leave a surface that could be worked on with a spokeshave and circular plane. I don't recommend this at all! It is a miracle that it ever got finished. Spokeshaving thick plywood edges is not a pleasant experience. Today, I would make an accurate template from something like Formica or hardboard, and template rout layers of MDF.

# Laminating the rail

I cut strips of birch ply with the outer grain at right angles to the length, so that they would bend more easily. Two strips were needed for each layer. These strips and the former were about ½in (12mm) taller than the finished rail. I needed to locate each pair of strips on the circumference of the jig, so that the ends would join in the right place. The first few layers meet in the waste area of the bridle joints, as do the last. The joins of each layer are staggered, so the second layer joins in a different pair of bridle joint to the first. A stout waxed nail, with the head removed, was inserted into either end of the jig. A slightly larger hole was drilled in each ply strip, to provide the location.

**Far left: A headless nail locates the laminates on the circumference of the rail.**

**Centre: A crude clamping with web clamps, G-clamps and soft block.**

**Left: Scribing lines with an engineer's height gauge.**

The clamping was done with a combination of three Stanley web clamps, and stout blocks lined with insulation board 'softening'. These blocks were applied after the web clamps, and held with large G-clamps and F-clamps. The whole set up was extremely crude, being largely dictated by lack of kit. I am astonished that it worked so well and would certainly design a more precise method today. The Tage Frid method shown on pages 5–7 of my second book (*David Charlesworth's Furniture-Making Techniques Volume Two*) would be ideal.

## Glue

I decided to use a urea formaldehyde glue (Aerolite) for its rigidity, slight gap-filling properties and long open assembly time. After some dry runs I found that I could comfortably glue three layers at a time, and eventually did three glue-ups in one day. There was considerable squeeze out and it is essential to wax and line everything with polythene, so that your job does not end up firmly glued to the bench. I managed to pull the two waxed nails out with a mole wrench, before gluing the last laminate layer.

When the laminating was completed, I left the rail on the former and scribed trimming lines near the top and bottom edges, with an engineer's height gauge, from my flat bench surface. I cut close to this line, with a tall fence on a circular saw. This method is illegal today, so I would devise a simple router jig to machine away the waste (see diagram). The router jig would run on the flat surfaces of the former, mounted on two MDF boards so that the top edge of laminated rail may be machined to the scribe line.

## Edges

I planed the top and bottom edges of the rail to perfect the surfaces. The blunting effect of the glue meant constant resharpening. The inner and outer vertical surfaces were also checked and worked on to remove some of the variations, which crept in during laminating.

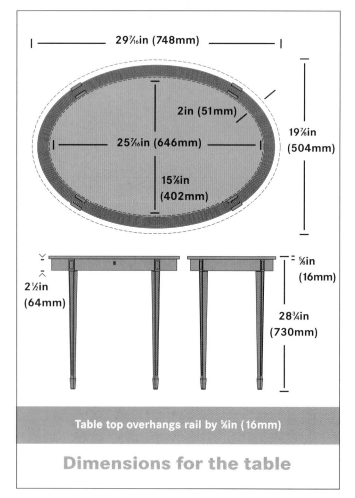

29⅜in (748mm)

2in (51mm)

25⅜in (646mm)

19⅞in (504mm)

15⅞in (402mm)

⅝in (16mm)

2½in (64mm)

28¾in (730mm)

**Table top overhangs rail by ⅝in (16mm)**

**Dimensions for the table**

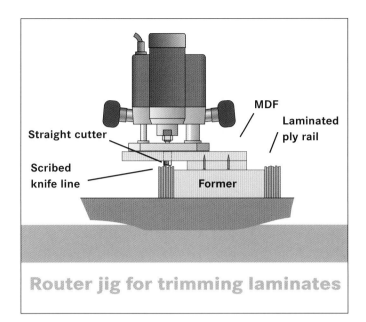

Straight cutter

Scribed
knife line

MDF

Laminated
ply rail

Former

**Router jig for trimming laminates**

## Crossbanding

The rosewood crossbanding on the top was laid with hot glue and trimmed with a cutting gauge, after the glue had gelled – the edges were veneered first.

The aim is to keep the grain lines at right angles to the edge of the curved top, so the sections get shorter and shorter towards the ends where the curve is tightest. This applies to all the horizontal surface crossbanding. The exception is the underside edge of the rail which I veneered with sycamore.

The narrow mahogany crossbanding was tailored on the edge which abutted the rosewood. As long as the gap is less than the thickness of your inlay line, the cutting in of the line will tidy it up. The face of a beech-cutting gauge was modified to sit securely on the curved edge of the ellipse.

## Bridle joints

The bridle joint positions had been transferred from the accurate drawing, which existed on the baseboard of the former, as the rail was being removed from the former. In laminated work it's often necessary to use the former as a rod or master drawing, as there are no face sides, edges or centre lines on the curved component. I marked some of these crucial details onto the inside face of the rail, with a chisel-sharpened 2H pencil. From these lines the rest of the bridle joints were also marked in pencil.

When everything had been checked, I laid the fiddleback veneer on the rails with hot glue, trimming back the long edges with a cutting gauge for the crossbanding. The vertical edges were cut with a set square and knife. The crossbanding was applied with gluefilm (see page 134) and the surfaces were sanded and refined, before cutting the bridle joints. I knifed the joint lines by using a 'thin leg sample', clamped to the inside surface of the rail. This supported a small engineer's set square on the inside curve, as well as defining the width. I made the joint one sheet of paper wider at the bottom than the top. This minute taper was a great help when the legs were finally fitted, done by planing the non-face edge of the leg to fit.

**Right top: Original veneer pictured next to the veneer that has faded over time.**

**Right bottom: Extra-fine inlay lines, badly faded and almost invisible.**

## Conclusion

Despite reservations about the inlay lines in the leg and the radius of the spade foot (see box, page131), I think this is one of my favourite pieces. I doubt the first few were profitable, but the customers liked them.

# Conversion tables

## millimetres to inches

| mm | inch | mm | inch | mm | inch | mm | inch |
|---|---|---|---|---|---|---|---|
| 1 | 0.03937 | 26 | 1.02362 | 60 | 2.36220 | 310 | 12.20472 |
| 2 | 0.07874 | 27 | 1.06299 | 70 | 2.75590 | 320 | 12.59842 |
| 3 | 0.11811 | 28 | 1.10236 | 80 | 3.14960 | 330 | 12. 99212 |
| 4 | 0.15748 | 29 | 1.14173 | 90 | 3.54330 | 340 | 13.38582 |
| 5 | 0.19685 | 30 | 1.18110 | 100 | 3.93700 | 350 | 13.77952 |
| 6 | 0.23622 | 31 | 1.22047 | 110 | 4.33070 | 360 | 14.17322 |
| 7 | 0.27559 | 32 | 1.25984 | 120 | 4.72440 | 370 | 14.56692 |
| 8 | 0.31496 | 33 | 1.29921 | 130 | 5.11811 | 380 | 14.96063 |
| 9 | 0.35433 | 34 | 1.33858 | 140 | 5.51181 | 390 | 15.35433 |
| I0 | 0.39370 | 35 | 1.37795 | 150 | 5.90551 | 400 | 15.74803 |
| 11 | 0.43307 | 36 | 1.41732 | 160 | 6.29921 | 410 | 16.14173 |
| 12 | 0.47244 | 37 | 1.45669 | 170 | 6.69291 | 420 | 16.53543 |
| 13 | 0.51181 | 38 | 1.49606 | 180 | 7.08661 | 430 | 16.92913 |
| 14 | 0.55118 | 39 | 1.53543 | 190 | 7.48031 | 440 | 17.32283 |
| 15 | 0.59055 | 40 | 1.57480 | 200 | 7.87401 | 450 | 17.71653 |
| 16 | 0.62992 | 41 | 1.61417 | 210 | 8.26771 | 460 | 18.11023 |
| 17 | 0.66929 | 42 | 1.65354 | 220 | 8.66141 | 470 | 18.50393 |
| 18 | 0.70866 | 43 | 1.69291 | 230 | 9.05511 | 480 | 18.89763 |
| 19 | 0.74803 | 44 | 1.73228 | 240 | 9.44881 | 490 | 19.29133 |
| 20 | 0.78740 | 45 | 1.77165 | 250 | 9.84252 | 500 | 19.68504 |
| 21 | 0.82677 | 46 | 1.81102 | 260 | 10.23622 | | |
| 22 | 0.86614 | 47 | 1.85039 | 270 | 10.62992 | | |
| 23 | 0.90551 | 48 | 1.88976 | 280 | 11.02362 | | |
| 24 | 0.94488 | 49 | 1.92913 | 290 | 11.41732 | | |
| 25 | 0.98425 | 50 | 1.96850 | 300 | 11.81102 | | |

1 mm = .03937 inch  1 inch = 25.4 mm
1 cm = 0.3937 inch  1 foot = 304.8 mm
1 m = 3.281 feet  1 yard = 914.4 mm

## inches to millimetres

| inch | | mm | inch | | mm | inch | | mm |
|---|---|---|---|---|---|---|---|---|
| 1/64 | 0.01565 | 0.3969 | 11/32 | 0.34375 | 8.7312 | 43/64 | 0.671875 | 17.0656 |
| 1/32 | 0.03125 | 0.7938 | 23/64 | 0.359375 | 9.1281 | 11/16 | 0.6875 | 17.4625 |
| 3/64 | 0.046875 | 1.1906 | 3/8 | 0.375 | 9.5250 | 5/64 | 0.703125 | 17.8594 |
| 1/16 | 0.0625 | 1.5875 | 25/64 | 0.390625 | 9.9219 | 23/32 | 0.71875 | 18.2562 |
| 5/64 | 0.078125 | 1.9844 | 13/32 | 0.40625 | 10.3188 | 47/64 | 0.734375 | 18.6531 |
| 9/32 | 0.09375 | 2.3812 | 27/64 | 0.421875 | 10.7156 | 3/4 | 0.750 | 19.0500 |
| 7/64 | 0.109375 | 2.7781 | 7/16 | 0.4375 | 11.1125 | 49/64 | 0.765625 | 19.4469 |
| 1/8 | 0.125 | 3.1750 | 29/64 | 0.453125 | 11.5094 | 25/32 | 0.78125 | 19.8438 |
| 9/64 | 0.140625 | 3.5719 | 15/32 | 0.46875 | 11.9062 | 51/64 | 0.796875 | 20.2406 |
| 5/32 | 0.15625 | 3.9688 | 31/64 | 0.484375 | 12.3031 | 13/16 | 0.8125 | 20.6375 |
| 11/64 | 0.171875 | 4.3656 | 1/2 | 0.500 | 12.700 | 53/64 | 0.828125 | 21.0344 |
| 3/16 | 0.1875 | 4.7625 | 33/64 | 0.515625 | 13.0969 | 27/32 | 0.84375 | 21.4312 |
| 13/64 | 0.203125 | 5.1594 | 17/32 | 0.53125 | 13.4938 | 55/64 | 0.858375 | 21.8281 |
| 7/32 | 0.21875 | 5.5562 | 35/64 | 0.546875 | 13.8906 | 7/8 | 0.875 | 22.2250 |
| 15/64 | 0.234375 | 5.9531 | 9/16 | 0.5625 | 14.2875 | 57/64 | 0.890625 | 22.6219 |
| 1/4 | 0.250 | 6.3500 | 37/64 | 0.578125 | 14.6844 | 29/32 | 0.90625 | 23.0188 |
| 17/64 | 0.265625 | 6.7469 | 19/32 | 0.59375 | 15.0812 | 59/64 | 0.921875 | 23.4156 |
| 9/32 | 0.28125 | 7.1438 | 39/64 | 0.609375 | 15.4781 | 15/16 | 0.9375 | 23.8125 |
| 19/64 | 0.296875 | 7.5406 | 5/8 | 0.625 | 15.8750 | 61/64 | 0.953125 | 24.2094 |
| 5/16 | 0.3125 | 7.9375 | 41/64 | 0.640625 | 16.2719 | 31/32 | 0.96875 | 24.6062 |
| 21/64 | 0.1328125 | 8.3344 | 21/32 | 0.65625 | 16.6688 | 63/64 | 0.984375 | 25.0031 |
| | | | | | | 1 | 1.00 | 25.4 |

# Suppliers

**Axminster Power Tool Centre Ltd**
Unit 10, Weycroft Avenue
Axminster
Devon
EX13 5PH
tel: 0800 371 822
**www.axminster.co.uk**

**Classic Hand Tools Ltd**
77 High Street
Needham Market
Suffolk
IP6 8AN
tel: 01449 721327
**www.classichandtools.com**

**Craft Supplies Ltd**
The Mill
Millers Dale
Nr Buxton
Derbyshire SK17 8SN
tel: 01298 871636
**www.craft-supplies.co.uk**
(Art Veneers is now part of Craft Supplies)

**Diamond Machining Technology (DMT)**
85 Hayes Memorial Drive
Marlborough
MA 01752
USA
tel: 508 481 5944
**www.dmtsharp.com**

**Dick Fine Tools**
Donaustr. 51
94526, Metten
Germany
tel: + 49 991 910930
**www.dick-gmbh.de**

**Dycem**
Suppliers of sticky rubber mats,
see page 87
**www.dycem.com**

**The Japan Woodworker**
1731 Clement Avenue
Alameda
California 94501
USA
tel: 510 521 1810 or 1 800 537 7820
**www.japanwoodworker.com**

**Lie-Nielsen Toolworks**
P.O. Box 9
Warren
ME 04864-0009
USA
tel: 207 273 1520
**www.lie-nielsen.com**

**Thanet Tool Supplies**
The Craftsman's Choice
New Ashford Market
Monument Way
Orbital Park, Sevington
Ashford, Kent
TN24 OHB
tel: 01233 501010
**www.shokunin.com**

**Tilgear**
Bridge House
69 Station Road
Cuffley, Potters Bar
Hertfordshire
EN6 4TG
tel: 01707 873434

# Further reading

David Charlesworth, *David Charlesworth's Furniture Making Techniques* (GMC Publications, 1999)

David Charlesworth, *David Charlesworth's Furniture-Making Techniques: Volume 2* (GMC Publications, 2001)

Garrett Hack, *The Handplane Book* (Taunton, 1997)

R. Bruce Hoadley, *Understanding Wood* (Taunton, 2000)

Ernest Joyce, *The Technique of Furniture Making* (Batsford, 1970)

Jim Kingshott, *Making and Modifying Woodworking Tools* (GMC Publications, 1992)

Leonard Lee, *The Complete Guide to Sharpening* (Taunton, 1995)

Thomas Lie-Nielsen, *Taunton's Complete Illustrated Guide to Sharpening* (Taunton, 2004)

Alan Peters, *Cabinetmaking – The Professional Approach* (Stobart, 1984)

Robert Wearing, *Making Woodwork Aids & Devices* (GMC Publications, 1999)

Robert Wearing, *The Resourceful Woodworker* (Batsford, 1996)

## About the Author

David Charlesworth runs private courses on the making of fine furniture from his home and workshop at Hartland in north Devon. He trained with Edward Baly, the principal founder member of the Devon Guild of Craftsmen, then turned from making commissioned pieces to teaching.

He regularly contributes articles to *Furniture & Cabinet Making* magazine, from which this collection was compiled, and is making a series of DVDs with Lie-Nielsen on hand tool techniques.

Details of his courses can be obtained by contacting David directly as follows:

Tel: (UK) 01237 441288
Email: davidcharl@aol.com
Website: **www.davidcharlesworth.co.uk**

## Acknowledgments

Many thanks to the staff at *Furniture & Cabinet Making* and my editors Virginia Brehaut and Gill Parris. None of this would have been possible without Pat's support, Bob Seymour's excellent photography and I am grateful to Simon Rodway for interpreting my rough sketches.

# Index

**For a complete catalogue or to place an order, contact:**
GMC Publications, Castle Place, 166 High Street,
Lewes, East Sussex BN7 1XU United Kingdom
Tel: 01273 488005 Fax: 01273 402866
Website: **www.gmcbooks.com**
Orders by credit card are accepted